QUALITY
in
LEARNING

A Capability Approach in
Higher Education

EDITED BY

John Stephenson & Susan Weil

KOGAN
PAGE

First published in 1992

Kogan Page Limited
120 Pentonville Road
London N1 9JN

British Library Cataloguing in Publication Data

A CIP record for this book is available from the British Library

ISBN 0 7494 0699 2

Typeset by Paul Stringer, Watford
Printed and bound in Great Britain by
Clays Ltd, St Ives plc

Contents

Acknowledgements

The authors have received a great deal of assistance in the preparation of this book. In effect, the book represents a statement from the capability movement, interpreted by the authors. Considerable thanks are given to the following groups of people.

The RSA, including Marigold Coleman and Mark Goyder, Director of Programmes, for mounting and supporting the Higher Education for Capability (HEfC) project from 1988 to 1991, when most of the field work was completed.

The sponsors of the HEfC project: British Petroleum Ltd, British Telecom, City of London Corporation, Council for Industry in Higher Education, Council for National Academic Awards, Department of Employment, Department of Education and Science, Digital Equipment Company Ltd, IBM (UK) Ltd, Lucas Industries, Leeds Polytechnic.and the University of Leeds.

Members of the HEfC Steering Committee: Christopher Price, Director of Leeds Polytechnic (Chairman); Sir Hermann Bondi, formerly Master of Churchill College, Cambridge; Ann Bailey, HE Manager, Digital Equipment Co. Limited; Patrick Coldstream, Director, Council for Industry and Higher Education; Geoffrey Harding, Academic Relations, IBM UK Ltd; Dr David Kirby, Durham University; Paul Litchfield, Department of Employment; Jeremy Nicholls, Education Liaison, BP PLC; Rev Canon Dr George Tolley, formerly Principal of Sheffield City Polytechnic; Professor John Tomlinson, Director, Institute of Education, University of Warwick and Chairman of RSA Council 1989–91; Professor Dorothy Wedderburn, Senior Fellow, Management School, Imperial College, formerly Principal, Royal Holloway and Bedford New College and Mike D. Yates, Enterprise in Higher Education, Department of Employment.

Leeds Polytechnic and the University of Leeds for facilitating the continuation of the Higher Education for Capability project.

The Enterprise in Higher Education Initiative – Anthea Weale, HEfC Enterprise Manager; Enterprise Directors; Higher Education Advisors, and Officers of the Department of Employment – for their continual help and support.

The Vice Chancellors, Polytechnic Directors, and College Principals who participated in private briefings at the RSA, invited the project Directors to their institutions and encouraged colleagues to submit examples.

The very many individuals and groups who submitted examples and comments, not all of whom it has been possible to quote directly despite their obvious relevance and quality.

The many people who participated in discussions at the RSA on each of the specialist areas included in Part Two and on the employers and professions sections in Chapter Nine.

The colleagues and friends who read and commented on early drafts.

The administrative staff of the RSA who provided excellent support at all stages: Sylvie Allisse, Cheryl Anderson, Rachael Boulton, Judith Corby, Linda Jackson and Lesley James.

The staff of the Higher Education for Capability project at Leeds who checked the detail and co-ordinated the work of the authors: Helen Pearson and Naomi Wilds.

The co-authors of the specialist chapters who did so much to cut through the volumes of material collected by the project.

Our personal friends and partners who tolerated our absorption in our work with good grace and who encouraged us to see it to completion.

Whilst the views expressed in the chapters are those of the named authors, the editors acknowledge the advice and comments given by the following people:

Art and Design

David Anderson, The Victoria and Albert Museum; Sylvia Aytoun, Wallis Fashion Groups Ltd; Linda Ball, Brighton Polytechnic; Professor Bruce Brown, Brighton Polytechnic; Anne Channon, Researcher/Writer Art and Design Education; Mike Ginsborg, Birmingham Polytechnic; Simon Lewis, Polytechnic of East London; Professor John Miles, Royal College of Art; Mr Wally Olins, The Wolf Olins Business; Gerda Roper, Newcastle upon Tyne Polytechnic; Terence Altham, International Wool Secretariat; Ann Tyrell, Ann Tyrell Design;

Business Management

Professor Peter Abell, London School of Economics; Mick Broadbent, Sheffield City Polytechnic; Thomas Clarke, University of St Andrews; Dr Ian Cunningham, Roffey Park Management College; Leslie Dickinson, Moray House College; Laurie Wood, University of Salford; Peter Goulden, Sunderland Polytechnic; Dr Roderick Gunn, Polytechnic of Wales, Bill Johnston, University of Strathclyde; Ann Latham, Wolverhampton Polytechnic; Steve Leary, Teesside Polytechnic; Andy Maslen, Staffordshire Polytechnic; Dr Richard Thorpe, Manchester Polytechnic; Dr Jean Whittaker, International Management Centre; Alexander Young, Heriot-Watt Business School;

Engineering/Technology

Mr Bill Peebles, Paisley College of Technology; Mr Leighton McDonald, Napier Polytechnic; Dr Judy Wilkinson, University of Glasgow; Mr Andrew Johnson, Sheffield University; Mr Alun Hughes, Staffordshire Polytechnic; Dr John Torry, University of Sussex; Professor Maurice Bonney, University of Nottingham; Mr Alan Davidson, University of Dundee; Mr Mike Laycock, Polytechnic of East London; Miss Yvonne T. Jenkins, Brighton Polytechnic; Ms Pamela Morton, Thames Polytechnic; Mr Peter Unstead, Polytechnic of East London; Mr Frank Curragh, Queens University Belfast;

Humanities and Social Sciences

Mr John Ibbeu, Kingston Polytechnic; Mr Patrick Coldstream, Council for Industry and HE; Ms Thelma Wilson, Polytechnic of East London; Mr Ken Carter, Coventry Polytechnic; Professor Paul Waddington, Birmingham Polytechnic; Professor Geoffrey Hurd, Wolverhampton Polytechnic; Professor Graham Chesters, Hull University; Dr G. F. Smith, University of Sterling; Ms Heather Eggins, CNAA; Dr Ron

Barnett, CNAA; Mr Hugh Robertson, Huddersfield Polytechnic; Dr Gail Davidson, City Polytechnic; Mr Peter Holmes, Thames Polytechnic; Dr Peter Bush, Glasgow College;

Science and Mathematics
Dr John Barkham, University of East Anglia; Mr F. B. Blakemore, The Polytechnic of Wales; Dr Douglas Buchanan, Moray House College; Dr R. P. Burn, Exeter University; Mr John C. Hughes, Imperial College; Ms Shiona McDonald, St Andrews College of Education; Dr Timothy Porter, University of Wales; Dr J. A. Rees, University of Manchester; Professor John E. Rees, University of Bath; Dr Stuart Spraggett, Coventry Polytechnic; Dr Ray Wallace, Nottingham Polytechnic;

Teacher Education
Dr E. B. Bates, Comino Foundation; Ms Anne Blanco, Thames Valley College of HE; Jose Chambers, INDTEL; Richard Dunne, University of Exeter; Professor J. Gilbert, University of Reading; Gareth Harvard, University of Exeter; Rob Hyland, Bedford College of HE; Julian Martin, Portsmouth Polytechnic; Dr Neil Moreland, Wolverhampton Polytechnic; Shirley Payne, Sheffield City Polytechnic; Brenda Smith, Nottingham Polytechnic; Gwydion Thomas, Ealing College of HE; Colin Walter, Goldsmith's College; Dr John Williams, The Engineering Council.

John Stephenson, Director, and Susan Weil, Associate Director

The Contributors

Professor David Bridges
David Bridges is Professor of Education at the University of East Anglia School of Education and Director of the Eastern Region Teacher Education Consortium in the Enterprise in Higher Education Initiative. He was previously Deputy Principal of Homerton College Cambridge.

Professor Tom Bromly OBE ATD FRSA
Tom Bromly is Dean of Arts and Design at Newcastle Polytechnic. He is a practising painter and photographer with works in a number of public and private collections. He has been chairman of the Conference for Higher Education in Art and Design (CHEAD), and chairman of the Trustees of the Art and Design Admissions Registry (ADAR).

Dr Ron Emanuel
Dr Emanuel is Academic Audit Officer at the University of Glasgow, was previously head of the Department of Chemistry and was the first director of the university's Enterprise in Higher Education project. He continues to teach chemistry.

Dr Philip Frame
Philip Frame is deputy head of the School of Management at the Business School, Middlesex Polytechnic. He has a faculty-wide responsibility for enterprise-related activities.

Professor Peter Lines MSc BSc(Hons) CEng FIEE MBIM
Peter Lines is Dean of the School of Engineering. He is a past chairman of the Committee for Engineering in Polytechnics and is currently a member of the Council for National Academic Awards and of the Initial Education and Training Committee of the Engineering Council.

Dr David Melling
David Melling is Dean of Humanities and Social Sciences at Manchester

Polytechnic. He is the author of the OPUS *Understanding Plato* and teaches ancient and Indian philosophy and Eastern Christian theology.

Professor John Stephenson, DPhil, BSc(Econ), PGCE, FRSA
Professor John Stephenson has been Director of the RSA's Higher Education for Capability project since September 1988. He was head of the School for Independent Study at North East London Polytechnic (now called Polytechnic of East London) from 1978 to 1988.

Dr Susan Weil
Susan Weil, Associate Director of the RSA Higher Education for Capability Initiative from 1989 to 1991, is now Head of Higher Education Development for the Office for Public Management, an independent body that offers stimulation and support for significant cultural change.

Dr John Williams BSc PhD CChem FRSC MBIM FRSA
John Williams joined The Engineering Council in 1986 and currently holds the post of Senior Executive – General Education, in which he is concerned with increasing the supply of engineers nationally into FE and HE.

Glossary

ACOST	Advisory Committee on Science and Technology
APEL	Accrediting Prior Experience and Learning
BTEC	Business and Technician Education Council
CAT	Credit Accumulation and Transfer
CATE	Committee for the Accreditation of Teacher Education
CNAA	Council for National Academic Awards
CQSW	Certificate of Qualification in Social Work
Dip HE	Diploma in Higher Education
DMS	Diploma in Management Studies
DTI	Department of Trade and Industry
EHE	Enterprise in Higher Education
GCSE	General Certificate of Secondary Education
HEfC	Higher Education for Capability
HEI	Higher Education Institution
HITECC	Higher Innovative Technology Engineering Conversion Course
HMI	Her Majesty's Inspectorate
HNC	Higher National Certificate
HND	Higher National Diploma
MBA	Master of Business Administration
MCI	Management Charter Initiative
NCVQ	National Council for Vocational Qualifications
PCFC	Polytechnics' and Colleges' Funding Council
PGCE	Postgraduate Certificate in Education
QTS	Qualified Teacher Status
RPA	Record of Progress and Achievement
RSA	Royal Society for the encouragement of Arts, Manufacturers and Commerce
SCE	Scottish Certificate in Education
SCOTVEC	Scottish Vocational Education Council
SML	Self-Managed Learning
TQM	Total Quality Management
TVEI	Technical and Vocational Education Initiative
UDACE	Universities' Council for Adult and Continuing Education

UDACE   Unit for the Development of Adult and Continuing Education
UFC   Universities Funding Council

Preface

In 1979, the Royal Society for the encouragement of Arts, Manufacturers and Commerce (RSA) issued the *Education for Capability Manifesto*.

EDUCATION FOR CAPABILITY
There is a serious imbalance in Britain today in the full process which is described by the two words 'education' and 'training'. The idea of the 'educated' person is that of a scholarly individual who has been neither educated nor trained to exercise useful skills; who is able to understand but not to act. Young people in secondary or higher education increasingly specialize, and do so too often in ways which mean that they are taught to practise only the skills of scholarship and science. They acquire knowledge of particular subjects, but are not equipped to use knowledge in ways which are relevant to the world outside the education system.

This imbalance is harmful to individuals, to industry and to society. A well-balanced education should, of course, embrace analysis and the acquisition of knowledge. But is must also include the exercise of creative skills, the competence to undertake and complete tasks and the ability to cope with everyday life; and also doing all these things in co-operation with others.

There exists in its own right a culture which is concerned with doing, making and organizing and the creative arts. This culture emphasizes the day-to-day management of affairs, the formulation and solution of problems and the design, manufacture and marketing of goods and services.

Educators should spend more time preparing people in this way for a life outside the education system. The country would benefit significantly in economic terms from what is here described as Education for Capability.

Education for Capability was created out of frustration at the artificiality of the divide between 'education' and 'training'. What was needed, the founders argued, was a new concept of education, one which respected the best features of each tradition, which developed people who 'can do' as well as who 'know about'.

The Capability Manifesto struck an immediate chord among educationalists, industrialists, community leaders and politicians of all parties. Support and monies were pledged and a national campaign was started.

During the early and mid-1980s, the RSA sought out, publicized and gave formal recognition to examples of capability education in practice. Teachers and students in schools, colleges, universities and polytechnics were invited to present their activities to 'the great and the good' assembled once a year at the RSA's Headquarters in London. These 'capability days', as they were called, contributed greatly to the debates which led to the curriculum reforms and initiatives of the 1980s. The Training and Vocational Education Initiative (TVEI), Enterprise in Higher Education (EHE), The National Record of Achievement, Core Skills and the General Certificate of Secondary Education (GCSE) all have what Professor Charles Handy describes as 'the fingerprints of the RSA all over them'.

With some notable exceptions, higher education remained sceptical about the relevance of the capability movement. Some saw it as an attack on traditional educational values; others thought it more relevant to education in schools and colleges. Indeed, the lack of response from higher education was cited by many schools as a reason why their mainstream work leading to university and polytechnic entry was largely unaffected by the capability debate.

In 1988 therefore, the RSA established a new three-year project, Higher Education for Capability (HEfC), to take the debate directly into the universities and polytechnics. Sponsorship was supplied by major companies and the Department of Employment, reflecting a widely held view of the time that higher education was not producing the kind of graduates needed for the challenges of the world of work. Sponsors of that first HEfC project included BP, IBM (UK) Ltd, Digital Equipment Co. Limited, The City of London Corporation, and the Department of Employment. The project worked in close parallel with the EHE initiative.

There have been substantial changes in the administrative, financial and political contexts within which higher education operates since Higher Education for Capability was established. Each has had an impact on the way higher education perceives its role, has made it more receptive to the original *Education for Capability Manifesto*, and has raised awareness of the need to address the issue of quality of provision. Among the more significant changes are:

- the formal linking of annual allocations of central Government funding to assessments of quality;

- the abolition of the Council for National Academic Awards (CNAA) with the loss of its role of monitoring programme and institutional quality;
- the transformation of the polytechnics into self-validating institutions;
- the introduction of academic audit procedures, focused on quality assurance;
- the growing importance of student fees as a major source of institutional income, promoting the status of the student as consumer;
- the substantial expansion of student numbers without commensurate expansion of resources;
- the widening of access into higher education to include groups traditionally under-represented, on the basis of a greater variety of previous educational experience;
- greater interest in partnership between employers and higher education; and
- the introduction of the Department of Employment's Enterprise in Higher Education Initiative.

The net effect of these changes has been to heighten interest in quality issues, whether to find ways of maintaining quality despite tighter student/staff ratios and scarce learning resources, to cope with a greater variety of student needs, to attract sponsorship from employers, to secure good quality ratings for central funding, to respond to pressure from students or simply to improve educational practice.

EHE has been particularly effective in encouraging debate and promoting changes in favour of the development of student personal skills and qualities. The Committee of Directors of Polytechnics and the Committee of Vice-Chancellors and Principals have initiated schemes to raise the quality of teaching, the National Council for Vocational Qualifications has begun to focus attention on the comparability of learning outcomes and different levels of attainment, Her Majesty's Inspectorate's reports on quality of courses have been used in assessing financial allocations to the polytechnics, and many institutions are considering the introduction of quality control systems such as British Standard 5750 or total quality management.

Throughout this period HEfC has maintained its focus on the quality and relevance of educational provision, urging the development of student capability through giving students greater responsibility for their own learning, and requiring students to explore and explain its relevance to their own development and to the wider community. The project discovered that many in higher education were willing to embrace this particular concept of student capability because they could see how it could: (1) give students a greater sense of ownership of their studies, (2) promote greater understanding of underlying principles, and (3) develop relevant qualities and skills in students. By August 1991 HEfC had participated in discussions in 70 higher education institutions, held 20 consultations with specialist interest groups, had established specialist networks of academic staff with experience of developing student capability within their own areas of study and had received details of over 400 examples of higher education for capability in practice.

This book explores the issue of quality in higher education in the context of an education for capability approach. In particular, it sets out the case for our emphasis on giving students, as individuals and in association with others, more responsibility and accountability for their own learning, and draws on the experiences of the many people from all kinds of institutions who are trying to bring it about. The major section of this book, Part Two, presents a picture of current activities within different subject areas, focusing on the educational issues raised, obstacles encountered and ways forward. We conclude with a review of some of the issues raised though current practice, and set out recommendations for actions which will help the increasing number of interested institutions to bring about lasting and effective change.

Sir John Harvey-Jones said this about Higher Education for Capability:

> All of us know that academic knowledge is not enough. What is needed is the capacity for making things happen and this requires a broader concept of education than pure academic achievement.
>
> To develop the highest levels of capability in our people is, without question, the single most important step that our country can take in the years ahead.

It is our view that the development of capable graduates is an aspiration of the highest order, and its achievement a genuine mark of quality in higher education.

Part One: The Context

Chapter One
Capability and Quality in Higher Education

John Stephenson

The quality of purpose
From the outset, the Higher Education for Capability (HEfC) project has been concerned about the purpose of higher education. The original *Education for Capability Manifesto* focused on the limited value of education which is solely in pursuit of knowledge and intellectual skills for its own sake. Individuals, industry and society as a whole benefit, the Manifesto asserted, when all of us have the capacity to be effective in our personal, social and working lives. This involves a much broader range of purposes than just the traditional concern for knowledge and intellectual skills. Higher education should be judged by the extent to which it: (1) gives students the confidence and ability to take responsibility for their own continuing personal and professional development; (2) prepares students to be personally effective within the circumstances of their lives and work; and (3) promotes the pursuit of excellence in the development, acquisition and application of knowledge and skills. Higher education will need to be able to achieve these interrelated purposes within the context of expanding numbers, diminishing resources and external accountability, and with an increasingly diverse mixture of students.

Capability – a working definition
Capability does not easily lend itself to detailed definition. It is easier to recognize it than to measure it with any precision. It is an integration of confidence in one's knowledge, skills, self-esteem and values. We have found widespread support for our resistance to the temptation to define capability in reductionist terms, seeking ever more separately measurable competences. Capability depends much more on our confidence that

we can effectively use and develop our skills in complex and changing circumstances than on our mere possession of those skills.

The following definition of capability, however, has been useful in exploring the essence of capability with academics:

> Capable people have confidence in their ability to (1) take effective and appropriate action, (2) explain what they are about, (3) live and work effectively with others and (4) continue to learn from their experiences, both as individuals and in association with others, in a diverse and changing society.

Capability is a necessary part of specialist expertise, not separate from it. Capable people not only know about their specialisms, they also have the confidence to apply their knowledge and skills within varied and changing situations and to continue to develop their specialist knowledge and skills long after they have left formal education.

Values, self-esteem and a commitment to learning

Capability is not just about skills and knowledge. Taking effective and appropriate action within unfamiliar and changing circumstances involves judgements, values, the self-confidence to take risks and a commitment to learn from the experience. Involving students in the decisions which directly affect what they learn, and how they learn it, develops a sense of ownership and a high level of motivation.

Many academics find the emphasis on confidence, esteem and personal values as well as on knowledge and skills relevant to their perception of an educated person and the role of higher education. Each of the four 'abilities' is itself an integration of many component skills and qualities, and each 'ability' relates to the others. For instance, one's ability to take *appropriate* action is related to one's specialist expertise which in turn is enhanced by one's learning from one's experiences of actions taken earlier. 'Explaining what one is about' involves much more than the possession of oral and written communication skills; it requires self-awareness and confidence in one's specialist knowledge and skills, and how they relate to the circumstances in hand.

Educating for capability through higher education

Capability, we argue, is developed as much by the way students learn as by what they learn. If students 'have experience of being responsible and accountable for their own learning, within a rigorous and interactive environment', they will develop confidence in their ability to take effective and appropriate action, to explain what they are about, to live and work effectively with other people, and to continue to learn from their own experiences. The medium, as they say, is the message. The Higher Education for Capability approach is a total approach. Confidence in one's personal qualities and specialist expertise is developed through successfully taking responsibility and accounting for the reflective application of specialist knowledge and skills.

The separate development of capability – often referred to as 'bolt-on capability' – has some superficial appeal. There are many well-constructed 'bolt-on' approaches in use but they always raise difficulties. They imply that normal educational activities are not about the development of personal qualities; they give students the impression that such activities are marginal, not central; and they set up timetable conflicts in which subject teaching will be more likely to prevail. When divorced from the students' academic studies, transferable skills raise issues of level, such as 'What is a good upper second class honours degree in listening skills?', thereby rendering them unsuitable for inclusion in the formal assessments leading to the award of degrees. The fundamental objection to the bolt-on approach, however, is that it denies the holistic nature of capability, the essential integration of personal qualities, skills and specialist knowledge which enables students to be effective. Communication, team-working and objective-setting, Higher Education for Capability argues, all have meaning when set within the student's educational interests and can enrich the student's specialist studies. The specialist context provides both the opportunity and the rationale for the development of personal skills and qualities.

The relevance of capability

To appreciate the value of student capability as an appropriate outcome for higher education, it is useful to explore its relevance to the world outside the seminar and lecture room. Three aspects are particularly relevant: feedback on the quality of graduates; uncertainty and change in society and the work-place; and the growing importance of individual responsibility and interdependence.

Feedback on graduate quality

One criticism of higher education voiced frequently by employers is that graduates are often lacking in a range of personal qualities and skills relevant to the world of work, including specific skills such as writing ability (a criticism often made of scientists and engineers) and numeracy (a criticism often made of humanities graduates) and general skills such as personal presentation and oral communication. More substantial criticisms extend to inadequacies in overall personal capabilities, often expressed in common-sense terms such as 'having nothing about them', 'not able to get on with things', 'no initiative and unreliable', 'unable to work well with others' and 'not able to cope with anything'.

Some of the more specific skills can be dealt with through intensive short-course training, minor changes in teaching methods and targeted feedback (eg, engineering students having their written reports corrected for clarity, grammar and spelling). The overall personal capabilities are of a higher order and require something much more substantial related to the very nature of students' overall educational experiences. The possession of transferable skills, like the possession of specialist knowledge, is no guarantee that a person will be able to use them effectively. Overall personal capability is an integration of diverse qualities, skills and knowledge.

Uncertainty and change in society and the work-place
Much of higher education practice has not caught up with the implications of preparing students for coping with uncertainty and change in the work-place. Teacher-dominated courses prepare inactive and passive learners for predictable situations; student responsibility and accountability helps students prepare for active participation in change. Figure 1 illustrates two contrasting contexts within which most graduates will have to operate.

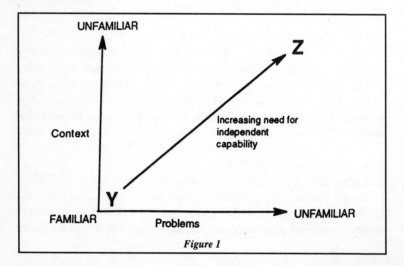

Figure 1

Most of us operate, for much of our time, in position Y on figure 1. In position Y, we are dealing with familiar problems for which we have learnt familiar solutions. The context in which we are operating is also familiar. Position Y can apply to the work-place, the home, community activities or artistic pursuits. Good performance in position Y may require technical skills and knowledge of the highest order or at the simplest level.

Insofar as our education beyond the age of 16 is a preparation for capability, it is mostly a preparation for position Y. We give students information about the context; the more complex the context, the more information we give them. We give them information about the kinds of problems they will meet, and details of the solutions which have been found to be effective. We might even give them practice in the implementation of the solutions and evaluation of their effectiveness. We seek to develop student capability in position Y by passing on other people's experience, knowledge and solutions. Though no doubt effective in the context of position Y, the resultant capability is essentially a dependent capability.

But position Y is not the whole of our experience. As indicated above, change is the order of the day. Many more of us will be spending more of our time having to operate in position Z. In position Z, we have less familiarity with the context and we have not previously experienced the problems with which we are faced. The slavish application of solutions perfected for familiar problems may have disastrous effects in position Z. To a large extent we are on our own, either individually or collectively. Very often, what distinguishes effective pilots, effective surgeons, effective social workers, effective teachers, effective builders and effective accountants is our confidence that they will eventually perform as well in position Z as in position Y.

Position Z is essentially a learning situation. By definition, we must inform ourselves about the unfamiliar context, not remind ourselves of what we were taught or trained to do. By definition, we must formulate the problems we have to deal with, not remind ourselves of problems previously learnt. We must devise solutions and ways of applying them, without the certainty of knowing the outcome, as a way of learning more about both the context and the problem. We need confidence in our ability to learn about the new context and to test possible ways forward from which we can learn. We need confidence in ourselves, and in our judgements, if we are to take actions in uncertainty, and to see initial failure as a basis of learning how to do better.

In position Z, intuition, judgement and courage become important; certainty based on proof and prior experience become less so. Specialist knowledge and skills are still relevant, but they are insufficient by themselves. It is necessary to appreciate their potential inadequacy, and to have the skills and confidence to enhance them. The solutions devised for the problems which are formulated will be essentially propositional in nature; developments from existing understanding. Evaluation of the consequences of actions taken in position Z will enhance our understanding and perhaps even improve our performance in position Y.

Preparing people to be effective in position Z is important at all levels of education. It is, however, of particular importance for higher education because it is from our graduates that many of our future leaders, in work as well as in the community, are likely to be drawn. As the intake to higher education expands and becomes more diversified, the more this will be true. The nation needs its future engineers, business executives, architects, social workers, administrators and citizens to be as capable in position Z as they are in position Y.

Individual responsibility and interdependence

By itself, coping with an accelerating rate of change in society and the work-place is not a sufficient basis on which to define the capability needed of graduates. It is also the nature of some of the changes in social and organizational structures which is putting a premium on individuals, in association with others, having more responsibility for managing their own affairs. New technology means that more people can work remotely from central control. New attitudes to organizations encourage flatter structures in which more people have direct responsibility for their own areas of activity, and for liaising and collaborating with contiguous activities, thus diminishing the more traditional hierarchical and authoritarian structures of control and communication. There are very few working situations in which team-working and effective communication with fellow workers, suppliers and clients are not crucial to success. Most specialists have to share their expertise with holders of related, or even different, expertise as a normal part of their working routine. Total quality management (TQM) requires all employees, as individuals or in teams, to examine their working practices and to promote changes leading to improved quality and/or efficiency. Squeezes on the public services enhance the importance of community groups, voluntary organizations and local activity; local management in schools, polytechnics, colleges and hospitals are part of this general trend towards spreading the burden of responsibility for their own development to a greater proportion of the community. On a more dramatic scale, the peoples of

Eastern Europe are having to learn that they too can take decisions affecting their own lives. We are moving very quickly towards what the RSA calls 'A Learning Society'. The more effectively more of us can take responsibility for our own personal and professional development, the more we as individuals, groups and nations will flourish.

Educating for capability and the quality of learning

Capability approaches to learning improve the quality of student learning by emphasizing the application of knowledge and skills, the negotiation of programmes, collaboration with others and structured reflection on progress.

Application of knowledge and skills: Rigid distinctions between the possession of knowledge and the application of knowledge are unhelpful. Reflections on the outcomes of actions can extend our knowledge or deepen our understanding; greater knowledge and deeper understanding can inform our planning and improve the effectiveness of our actions. Properly managed, action-based learning can be an effective way of testing what we know and improving what we do. Even the most abstract of academic specialisms, including art and philosophy, lend themselves to propositions, argument, challenge, application, learning from experience and the development of confidence in one's personal skills.

The negotiation of programmes: To prepare and secure agreement for programmes of study, students need to develop clarity of purpose, to communicate those purposes, to express their purposes as learning goals which can be achieved and demonstrated, and to show how what they propose to do is feasible in terms of time and resource availability. On most conventionally organized courses these highly educational activities are the preserve of the teacher.

Collaborative learning: This requires students to share roles and tasks which, in turn, requires awareness and acceptance of those tasks. There is access to a greater amount of data when students are able to pool their individual learning for the collective purpose. Pooling of learning requires students to communicate what they have learnt to peers and eventually to others, and the collaborative learning environment gives opportunity for the practice and development of their interpersonal skills.

Reflection on progress: Learner responsibility and accountability promote *deep learning*, taking students into a search for meaning and for
underlying principles. Students have to judge the relevance of what they
learn to their longer term goals. As they do so, they are able to integrate
the various components of their studies in their own minds, around the
unity of their negotiated purpose. In the conventional course, meaning,
underlying principles, relevance and component integration are the
preserves of the teacher – if teacher teaches A, then A must be relevant
to the course. On capability programmes, students own their programmes
of study and internalize their learning experiences.

Many educational researchers have associated student responsibility
and accountability with strength of motivation and learning effectiveness. Sherman (1985), for instance, claims that 'when learners see
themselves as instrumental to achieving outcomes, they tend to gain
higher levels of attainment', a view based on 'the concept that learning
is a personal activity requiring personal learning decisions'. Knowles
(1986) asserts that 'learners generally need to understand... how it will
benefit them if they learn it' (p. 41) and that 'when they do understand,
there is a release of so much energy for the learning' (p. 37).

Biggs (1985) concludes that being able 'to exert control over their
own cognitive resources' is an important condition of deep learning
(Marton and Saljo, 1976) and recommends 'independent study' as a
strategy for its development (p. 210). Pask (1976) refers to 'holistic
learners' (p. 130) who 'assimilate information from many topics in order
to learn the "aim" topic' (p. 130), thereby becoming 'comprehensive
learners', capable of learning 'at a deep level' (p. 132). Lamdin and
Worby (1976) found that learning 'created of the student, by the student,
for the student' at Empire State College fostered 'a kind of intellectual
and emotional maturity' (p. 66), and Biggs (1979) argued that 'internal-
izing strategies' led to high level performance.

In summary, giving students opportunities to be responsible and
accountable for their own learning prepares them for effective performance in their personal and working lives, enhances their commitment to
their studies, promotes deeper understanding, builds confidence in their
ability to learn and helps the development of high-level personal qualities
and skills. In short, capability education is quality education.

Challenges
Introducing Higher Education for Capability presents challenges for
students, teachers, course designers, professional and accrediting bodies,

institutional managers and employers of college graduates. It is a major task. Circumstances, however, are becoming more favourable, particularly given:

(1) the realization that the rapid expansion of knowledge, particularly in business, engineering and science, cannot be accommodated within the confines of conventional timetables;
(2) higher student/staff ratios, which are encouraging many institutions to rethink their teaching strategies; and
(3) larger numbers of what used to be called 'non-standard students', causing institutions to introduce more flexible ways of responding to different student needs

Higher Education for Capability argues that helping students develop their independent capability is an aspiration of the highest quality. Its achievement demands a high level of commitment and invention on the part of the staff, flexibility on the part of the institution and support from external bodies. The educational challenge is to devise courses and invent learning experiences which help students to acquire the necessary expertise – both knowledge and skills – for effective performance in familiar and predictable circumstances in ways which give students confidence in their ability to cope equally effectively with uncertainty and change.

References

Biggs, J.B. (1979) 'Individual Differences and Study Processes and the Quality of Learning Outcome' *Journal of Higher Education,* 8, pp. 381–94.
Biggs, J.B. (1985) 'The Role of Meta-Learning in Study Processes' *British Journal of Educational Psychology* 55, pp. 185–212.
Knowles, M.S. (1986) *Using Learning Contracts.* San Francisco: Jossey-Bas.
Lamdin, L. and Worby, D. (1976) 'Across The Desk Learning Through Independent Study' *Alternative Higher Education* 1 (1), pp. 61–7.
Marton, K. and Saljo, R. (1976) 'On Qualitative Differences in Learning: 1 – Outcomes and Process' *British Journal of Educational Psychology*, 46 (1), pp. 4–11.
Pask, G. (1976) 'Styles and Strategies for Learning' *British Journal of Educational Psychology*, 46 (2), pp. 128–48.
Sherman, T. M. (1985) 'Learning Improvement Progress: A Review of Controllable Influences' *Journal of Higher Education*, 56 (1), pp. 85–100.

Chapter Two
Four Themes in Educating for Capability

John Stephenson and Susan Weil

Introduction
Taking responsibility and being accountable for their own learning involves students in four related groups of activities:

(1) reviewing and building on previous experience, knowledge and skills;
(2) preparing plans and negotiating approvals;
(3) active and interactive learning; and
(4) the assessment of performance according to agreed learning outcomes.

If the student's programme is to have coherence, it is important that the student engages in each of the four groups of activities, irrespective of subject specialism or whether the programme is an afternoon's exercise or a complete undergraduate course. The resultant course content, learning activities and forms of assessment are then related to the students' circumstances and are justified in terms of their relevance to the wider purposes of the course as a whole.

The four groups of activities, or themes, can recur in successive cycles with each assessment of performance providing a new platform on which to base further planning and negotiation. Where students consciously commit themselves to reflect on their learning from each of the themes, and their tutors see their role as helping them to do so, the quality of each successive cycle of activities is enhanced.

The brief summaries which follow are overviews of the four themes. They indicate some of the issues of practice and principle which need to be considered when contemplating the development of capability programmes and are intended to give the reader some points of reference when reading the specialist chapters in Part Two: The Experience which follows.

Theme One: Reviewing and building on experience

Overview of the theme
Starting at the point students have reached is almost a first principle of teaching. On conventionally taught courses, tutors' knowledge of the experience students bring with them often consists of generalizations based on scanty information about previous courses (eg, in schools or on earlier course components) and the performance of previous groups of students. Individual needs and aspirations may not be known and, therefore, maximization of individual benefit may be inhibited.

A number of factors are beginning to encourage teachers to look more closely at individual student differences within their courses. Modular structures, wider access, and different courses in feeder schools and colleges result in a greater variety of student experience and expertise within the same class or lecture hall, putting pressure on conventional delivery modes of teaching. Quality assessments based on value-added concepts of educational benefit require more systematic appraisals of student starting points.

When the students themselves take responsibility for appraising their own educational starting points, they take the first step in controlling their own educational development. Where appraisal of student experience is conducted with the help of others, including peers, academics and employers, students have the opportunity to test their judgements about themselves against the judgement of others, thereby helping them develop confidence in their ability to assess their relative strengths and aptitudes. A willingness to acknowledge one's weaknesses together with a well-founded confidence in one's strengths are a good start for self-development and provide a relevant basis on which to build one's plans.

Clarifying where you are starting from is educationally valuable and contributes greatly to the quality of learning. Student motivation is enhanced. Self esteem is raised as students begin to appreciate the value of their own experience and expertise. Evaluation, communication and team-working skills are developed. Time devoted to this activity, particularly if conducted within students' specialist studies, is not a diversion but an aid to understanding and commitment. It helps teachers to plan effective responses and support.

Some issues of principle and practice
Are students given prior information, and a clear rationale, before being asked to appraise their own experience? This is particularly important

where such schemes are introduced within more traditional educational environments.

Should student willingness towards, and potential for, taking responsibility be factors in the selection of students? Records of Achievement and Accreditation of Prior Experience and Learning techniques (APEL) will make this more feasible.

What techniques, materials, expertise and staff development support is available for teachers?

Are diagnostic tools available to help students arrive at objective assessments of their abilities? Do students have the opportunity to test their judgements about their expertise and to explore their potential areas of interest?

Is the process of appraising experience seen to be a learning experience in its own right?

How responsive is the programme or institution to the outcomes of appraisals? Are resources available and accessible to provide the extra support needed to deal with the gaps students identify? Is there sufficient flexibility in the programme for them to build on their strengths?

Theme Two: Planning, negotiation and approval

Overview of the theme

By itself, student self-determination is not a sufficient justification for the design of their programmes. Many other factors have to be taken into account, including possible professional or employment needs, the intellectual demands of the proposed areas of study, student expertise, public confidence in the level of the qualification being sought and the resources available, including tutorial support. Students need to be able to show how these constraints can be accommodated or overcome. Students have to be accountable as well as responsible for what they plan to do. Learner responsibility and accountability invariably mean negotiating approvals from other stakeholders.

The negotiation of programmes can apply to whole programmes or short-term activities, and can extend to any combination of the following: the content, the application of the content, the location, the resources used, the method of study, the mode of assessment and the criteria of assessment. Planning and negotiating approval for a programme of study or learning activity which is both personally relevant and externally valid, as explained in Chapter One, develops a deeper understanding of underlying principles and an awareness of the programme's wider relevance. Negotiation provides practical experience of objective setting, resource planning, oral and written communication, collaboration, deciding priorities and critical self-awareness. Students have to address key issues such as content integration and the criteria and mode of assessing their end performance.

The balance of power between the various parties to the negotiation is of crucial importance. In some cases, where there are externally imposed course requirements, the scope for negotiating course content and final assessment may be very limited. In others, agreements emerge from critical dialogue between the student and tutor. Students have most protection against more powerful parties when the procedures and areas for negotiation, the resource constraints and the criteria by which their proposals will be judged are clear and understood by all. If negotiation is reduced to students guessing what the tutor really wants them to do, the whole process is discredited.

Effective use is made of the opportunity to negotiate their own programmes when students receive advice, time and support for content mapping, resource exploration, programme construction and objective-setting. Staff help most when they provide a rigorous but supportive environment, and when they appreciate that time spent on planning and negotiating is at least as valuable as 'getting on with it' and, indeed, *is* getting on with it. Employers help most when they allow students to explore the job implications of what they intend to study and give access to relevant learning opportunities and resources at their disposal. Institutions help most when their learning resources are made directly accessible to students and where they minimize departmental and external barriers. Everyone helps when they examine closely their assumptions about what is or is not possible; a constraint may be no more than a custom or practice which has survived despite its original *raison d'être* having expired.

Some issues of principle and practice
Is there clarity about: (1) what is negotiable, (2) the procedures for the preparation and submission of plans, (3) the resources available and (4) the criteria for approval? Are the procedures, criteria and judgements formal or informal; are they implicit or explicit?

How can the course ensure that 'the basics' are covered? Is there a body of knowledge which is not negotiable?

How is the tension between student responsibility and teacher 'knowing best' resolved?

Is help given for process issues, for example, objective-setting, setting out proposals etc?

Are students given time and help to explore possible course content, employment needs and their existing expertise? Are 'taster courses' available? Are students helped to consider the importance of developing personal qualities and skills?

Are students encouraged to relate their proposals to their prior experience and longer term personal, academic and professional development?

Is the process of planning and negotiation seen as a learning experience for the student? Is formal credit given for the learning derived from the planning and negotiation of a major programme of study? Are students encouraged to renegotiate aspects of their programmes in the light of progress and unintended outcomes?

How are other key stakeholders – professional bodies, employers – involved, and do they help? By what means are student negotiated programmes externally validated?

What are the implications for teachers? What kind of staff development is needed to help tutors switch from formal teaching to helping students plan and negotiate their own programmes? Does it subvert their traditional role of being 'the authority'?

Is the institution flexible in its responses to student initiative? Are cross-discipline and extra-institutional programmes possible?

Theme Three: Active and interactive learning

Overview of the theme

Active and interactive learning are key features of educating for capability because they give students the opportunity to: (1) apply and test their knowledge and skills, (2) develop a range of personal skills and qualities, (3) relate their studies to the world outside, (4) gain experience of collaboration within a framework of specific objectives and (5) take initiatives and learn from their own experiences. Passive learning, characterized by the transmission of lecture notes for re-presentation in formal assessments, may inhibit the development of capability and encourage dependence on other people's learning. In terms of the four capability themes, active and interactive learning represent the carrying out of the programmes previously planned and negotiated by the student.

The range of possible activities is wide. It includes individually and collaboratively planned assignments, enquiries, projects, workshops, simulations, client-based consultancies and work-based learning. Active learning is not synonymous with practical work, much of which can be teacher dominated. It involves the student in explicit and critical reflection on issues and problems raised by initiatives students have taken, and the seeking of information and ideas to aid that reflection.

Active learning develops organizational and self-management skills. Successes boost confidence; participation and involvement raise motivation. Interactive learning develops interpersonal skills such as communication, leadership, task-sharing, the giving and receiving of criticism and the negotiation of individual contributions to common tasks. It involves students in constant explanations of their own learning and exposes them to the learning of other students. It can be both demanding and fun.

New roles are demanded of tutors, related to: (1) helping students to talk through what they are doing and what they have learnt, (2) structuring the intellectual and physical learning environment to provide rigour and support, (3) providing a focus on questions and process rather than answers and content, (4) giving constructive feedback on student performance against student learning goals, (5) giving access to specialist resources and expertise and (6) helping students to build up their awareness and understanding of their specialist fields.

Active and interactive learning do not preclude the use of lectures, formal instruction, teacher-prepared information, group and individual tutorials or extensive reading. What is important is that these traditional features of higher education are supportive of, and informed by, learning from activities negotiated and managed by the students themselves. Lectures can be useful when they are challenging, inspirational, context- setting or provide 'live' information on current issues which is not readily available elsewhere. They can be used in response to common problems experienced by students.

Formal instruction in basic skills can fill gaps identified through student appraisals of their own experience and learning. Tutorials provide a forum for open reflection and shared learning. Permanently available teacher-prepared material, like library-based materials, can provide a background level of information and conceptual support. Where lectures, formal instruction and teacher-prepared materials comprise and determine the whole of the course, they are unlikely to develop student capability; where they support and respond to student initiative, they can inform student reflection and aid the development of understanding. Capability programmes are teacher supported, not teacher dependent.

Active and interactive learning raise resource availability issues. Strong motivation makes it possible for many activities to proceed without direct supervision, releasing staff time for tutorials. Other learning resources need to be readily available; institutional services need to be responsive; employers and external clients can be sources of extra support.

Some issues of principle and practice

Do active and interactive learning take place within the context of the students' specialist studies, and do their purposes include both the enhancement of the student's understanding of the field and the development of personal skills and qualities?

How easily can staff switch from their traditional teaching roles? What kind of staff development works?

How do students working on different activities monitor their own progress?

How can staff monitor and facilitate the growth in student understanding and coverage of 'the knowledge base' derived from the activities?

Do employers and other outsiders get directly involved in student learning activities? Is the pool of learning material available to students greater than on a lecture-based programme?

Is time made available for critical reflection on the learning derived from the activity? Does learning from activities take precedence over participation in the activities? Is tutor feedback directed at student learning and the development of skills and qualities?

In interactive learning, is it possible to distinguish individual contributions and learning? Is tuition or guidance provided in the special skills involved in successful collaboration?

Is it possible to provide effective supervision and to monitor the learning in work-based learning?

Theme Four: Assessment

Overview of the theme

To be consistent with its aims, a capability course should assess student capability in the context of the students' specialist studies, which in turn means – according to the working definition of capability used by Higher Education for Capability – that assessment should give students opportunities to demonstrate:

(1) their grasp of their specialist studies through their ability to apply their knowledge and skills in relevant situations;

(2) their ability to explain what they have learnt, and discuss its relevance to their specialist field and their personal and professional development;

(3) their ability to work effectively with others, including students and potential colleagues or clients; and

(4) their ability to evaluate their own learning critically and to indicate how they might progress it further.

Successful demonstration of the above, *ipso facto*, also allows successful demonstration of a range of component personal skills related to interaction, oral and written communication, and evaluation, integrated with each other and with the students' specialist work. Preparing for capability assessments is, in itself, a valuable learning experience. Demonstrating one's capability to peers, tutors, potential employers, panels and external examiners can be a more rigorous assessment than the passing of unseen written examinations on teacher-provided information or the separate demonstration of isolated personal skills, as promoted by the competency movement. The skills and qualities necessary to complete such assessments are particularly relevant to the world outside; the ability to apply and critically review one's specialist knowledge indicates a high level of understanding of underlying principles of the students' specialist field. In total, capability assessments are quality assessments.

Despite their obvious relevance, capability assessments leading to the award of degrees are rare; their use for monitoring assessment and in non-contributory course components is more common. Three difficulties are frequently mentioned: (1) the assumed need to achieve comparability and statistical validity by giving all students the same course and the same assessment, (2) the identification of individual contributions within collaborative activities, and (3) the objectivity and reliability of self- and peer-assessments. Capability assessments, however, are about what students know and can do, judged against agreed criteria; they are not about ranked performance and comparability. If, as in the driving test, there are clear and universally applied criteria related to the general level of awards against which students can justify their proposed specialist objectives, the currency of the awards can be protected and the integrity of individual needs can be preserved. There does not seem to be a problem of principle with this approach at the doctorate level. Multiple sources of information on student performance are available when students demonstrate the application of their knowledge and skills outside the institution, ensuring the reliability as well as the relevance of the assessment. Individually negotiated objectives and critical reviews can identify individual contributions in group-assessments. The rationale offered by students for their self- and peer-assessments can be externally assessed; it is the student's ability to make appropriate judgements which matters.

Capability assessments describe what students have done or can do; they do not predetermine what students must learn. They provide a wide range of useful information about the student to anyone who needs to know. They are learning experiences.

Some issues of principle and practice
Is education for capability kept on the sidelines by the use of non-capability assessments for the final award?

What alternatives to the traditional unseen written examinations are available, and with what success? Is confidence in their objectivity addressed and, if so, how?

Are the *general* requirements for degrees – for example, the criteria related to the *level* of the award – clear and made available to students at the outset? Are students able to negotiate their *specific* learning goals and the –specific criteria by which they will be assessed? Is there discussion on the validity of the students' proposals?

How can social pressures on certain sub-groups (gender and ethnic minorities) be accommodated in the assessment of individual performance in groups?

What is the experience of involving non-academics, such as employers, clients and professional practitioners, in the formal assessment of student performance?

What is the feasibility of assessing large numbers of possibly idiosyncratic pieces of work?

How can a wide range of learning outcomes best be recorded and made available to those who need to know? What use is made of records of achievement, logs and portfolios? Can the recording of learning outcomes be done by the student?

Are students required to justify their self- and peer-assessments?

Part Two: The Experience

Introduction

In Part Two, we present a review of Higher Education for Capability in practice, based on an analysis of examples brought to our attention between 1988 and 1991. The scope of the review is inevitably constrained by the range submitted. Many excellent examples, no doubt, have escaped our attention. Nevertheless, we are confident that the ones we have received highlight important issues and suggest useful methods of proceeding.

The structure of the specialist chapters
The examples have been analysed according to a matrix of two sets of criteria, namely subject areas and education for capability processes.

The subject areas
We recognize that most academics in higher education have a strong empathy with their specialist field; many see the development of their subject as the primary focus for their teaching. They identify with fellow specialists rather than with educationalists and believe their subject area has distinctive characteristics which require distinctive modes of teaching. In recognition of the need to start where people are, the 1988 to 1991 Higher Education for Capability Project established networks of specialists drawn from six general areas: art and design, business and management, engineering and technology, humanities and social sciences, sciences and mathematics and teacher education. Examples were considered by network meetings at the RSA and the project directors and network conveners prepared the specialist chapters which follow.

The capability issues
The second set of criteria – key capability themes – cuts across all the subject areas. The four capability themes are outlined in Chapter Two.
The matrix of subject specialisms and capability themes enables subject teachers to explore education for capability within the context of

their own fields while facilitating cross-reference to capability experience in others. Readers interested in capability processes in general can explore their application across a range of subject areas.

Each specialist chapter has been prepared by a subject specialist and a Higher Education for Capability director, thus ensuring both dimensions are well represented. The chapters vary in style and emphasis according to the distinctive features of each subject area, the extent of the experience of educating for capability and the range of examples available and submitted. In some subjects, student responsibility and accountability are still rare. In art and design, however, promoting student self-development is considered a normal concern of most courses. The art and design chapter, therefore, presents a description of what the participants regard as typical student experiences; other chapters present reviews of distinctive and innovative examples.

Status of the examples

Where specific examples are featured in the text, they are not presented as exemplars or models of good practice (though they may be), but as sources of information about other people's experience. Not all of the examples illustrate all the four capability themes. They are reports from the field rather than case studies and are intended to offer a flavour of the different approaches to education for capability across a range of specialisms.

All examples which have contributed to the project are listed by institution at the end of the book. Reference numbers in the text, eg {26}, identify those examples quoted directly.

The future

The six specialist chapters are regarded as initial statements of the development of capability programmes in particular areas. The authors hope the chapters stimulate more institutions to submit examples and, as the pool of examples grows, they intend to prepare fuller publications devoted to particular subjects. Higher Education for Capability is also building up a national database of capability and enterprise experience. The database is available via the Joint Academic Network – a computer-based distribution system – or by writing to the HEfC office at 20 Queen Square, Leeds, LS2 8AF.

Chapter Three
Capability Through Art and Design

John Stephenson and Tom Bromly

The context

As a creative, practical and problem-solving activity, art and design education is well suited for the development of capability.

Visual images are effective means of communicating information, ideas, concepts and emotions. They have a major part to play in the shared formulation of problems and the exploration of solutions. They can convey innovative ideas and propositions in advance of the development of language relevant to those ideas and propositions. Visual intelligence is therefore a major feature of capability. We live in a society in which visual communication is dominant and its power is understood and exploited by skilled communicators. The whole of the man-made environment has a strong visual dimension and those lacking visual intelligence and understanding are at a disadvantage in that environment.

Modern technology, in the form of low-cost video cameras, cable networks, desk-top publishing, word-processing and electronic imagery, is giving many more people access to potentially effective visual media. Raising people's visual skills is as important as raising the more traditionally emphasized oral and written skills of communications.

Awareness of how visual material can be manipulated to suit the purposes of the communicator helps people understand and analyse the intentions behind the communication. Image interpretation is an important part of the full range of communication capability. Greater visual communication skills increase our ability to explain ourselves and to understand others. There are no language boundaries in visual communication which, depending on a shared cultural understanding, makes universal communication possible and available to all.

In the urban environment most artefacts are a result of some aspect of design thinking and decision making, be they the buildings we live in or the clothes we wear. Such decision making is not only the prerogative of the designer but of the user as well. Not only do we need to improve the production of these artefacts, but the users need to have a similar understanding to benefit from them. Awareness of the creative process involved enables the user to participate in the creation of the man-made environment, thus facilitating choice, collaboration and a shared desire for quality and fitness of purpose.

Capability features of art and design education

Art and design education sets out to develop individual abilities, skills and understanding through practice, set within an historical and cultural context. 'Live' practice encourages a concern for self-identified and project-specific problems as well as a search for solutions, and enhances creativity, invention and practical understanding.

The universal effectiveness of visual images means that art and design influences, and is influenced by, other social and cultural activities. Students extend their experience in a broad and evolving landscape and, as a consequence, their learning activities focus on the evaluation of their own progression not only amongst their immediate student peer group but also within the culture itself.

Learning through making requires critical awareness and self-evaluation to be developed in parallel with understanding. Content and process have to occur simultaneously for ideas to be expressed visually and materially. This duality is so central to the subject that, initially, much study time is taken up in enabling students to develop this facility. This may be a foundation year of study (something that has been formally recognized in art and design for some 30 years), a series of induction courses or part of an initial period of diagnostic study before specialization.

The strong emphasis on practice within art and design education enables professional artists and designers, together with representatives from those industries employing artists and designers, to participate in the student's learning process. This occurs in direct teaching situations, the setting and evaluation of professional projects, placement experience, residences and public exhibitions. Such dialogue and collaboration puts the student learning experience into a realistic context, establishing a professional and industrial environment for which most students are preparing themselves. The practitioner, as teacher, not only understands the nature of the learning experience in art and design but also understands and encourages the application of creative ideas to customer and client needs. Such experience is invaluable in providing a platform for professional development and a bridge between learning and practice.

The bridge with professional practice is extended through to assessment, where the external examiners include practising professionals able to evaluate the work of the student in a professional context. As each student's work is in itself a piece of research involving self-directed enquiry, it is appropriate that both the negotiation and completion of student work is so evaluated. Critical evaluation not only occurs within the assessment process but is central to the learning process, too, which can best be described as a process of constant critical dialogue between staff and student, student and student, and, finally, client and ex-student.

Art and design students, therefore, develop a facility for critical awareness as part of their own working methodology. They also employ it amongst their own student peer group both formally in project or group 'crits', and informally when discussing each other's work. Team learning also requires a shared critical perception which becomes the framework on which such group work is based. Students therefore learn from other students' mistakes and achievements as much as they do from their own.

Group learning is commonplace in art and design. Some activities such as film and video work require production teams to enable the work to materialize. Even when the work is concerned with an individual idea, that idea cannot take shape without the help of others (lighting, sound, camera, props, continuity, etc) and so a range of interactive skills and learning processes are required. By co-operation and interchange of activity, learning becomes a collective experience and is consequently more valuable.

Business understanding in art and design is best learnt when it is related to specific projects and is seen as part of the brief. Time-scales, production costs, promotional considerations and technical problems are all best understood when they are encountered in reality rather than in theory. For that reason, projects that are set by companies, or works that are site specific or are for a specific exhibition or showing, carry with them a discipline that incorporates other learning strategies.

Related studies such as the history of art and design, have more value when they are fully integrated with the main study. Rather than pursuing theoretical studies as a separate activity, students benefit by understanding how their own creative ideas relate to, and are shaped by, the culture of which their work is a part. The culmination of this integration can be witnessed in both the practical work and the written dissertation.

Current issues in art and design education
The success of art and design education in the UK is recognized and emulated world-wide. Many design students in particular are sought after

and employed in high profile companies in Europe, America and Japan. While it is often considered to be an expensive education in unit cost terms, this is not borne out when compared with other courses with practical elements in technology, science, medicine and architecture. It is cost effective in its ability to retain students – the wastage rate is minimal compared with the average – and it is one of the very few subjects in which students are expected to start employment in their specialist fields without further training. Although there is no employment identified specifically for the fine art student, the flexible and adaptable nature of their education, employing a number of capability skills, means that they are able to, and do, take up employment across a diversity of activities where their particular creative and visual thinking gives them a considerable advantage.

It is probable, however, that much that is good and valuable in art and design education – in fact the very nature of the education itself – could well be lost in the changes that are sweeping through higher education at the moment. A rapid increase in student numbers without a corresponding increase in financial support is making it almost impossible to continue to provide the learning climate that has supported such a successful education practice.

A move towards lecture-based mass education rather than individual learning through practical skill-based study, together with the apparent attractiveness of modular courses as an expedient, will devastate the very nature of art and design education as a specialist study and transform it into a liberal arts education that broadly informs but doesn't develop individual student potential. There has already been a severe cut back in the employment of practising artists and designers as specialist staff. Many specialisms are no longer available because of cost and a number of known art and design courses have been dissolved into institutional modular structures which encourage breadth rather than specialism.

These policies may well produce a greater participation in higher education, but at a cost. Unless the emerging broadly based education is endorsed by more specialist postgraduate education, then much of the proven success in art and design education may be lost and, with it, our ability to provide artists and designers of capability.

Theme One: Reviewing and building on experience
The art and design commitment to helping students take responsibility for their own educational and professional development begins at the

point of recruitment and admission and continues into the first stages of the course. Three features predominate: the foundation course; admission by negotiation and portfolios of students' work; and the early induction of students into taking responsibility.

Foundation courses

Most entrants to undergraduate courses in art and design come via a one-year full-time or two-year part-time foundation course which are run in a variety of institutions, including the polytechnics themselves. Foundation courses seek to give students experience of what it will be like for them when they join an undergraduate course. They provide a grounding in some essential skills and a range of experience on which students can base effective choices about their own professional development. They also provide a bridge between the heavily teacher-led environment of most schools to the student-led environment of art and design higher education. The first term of one polytechnic's foundation course {81}, for instance:

> ...is conceived as a general course that aims at introducing students to the various disciplines and modes of thinking embraced by different areas of study.

The explicit aim is to give students direct experience of the skills and qualities required in different specialisms and the means to appraise their abilities, so that they might have:

> ...the clearest possible picture, not only of the training involved on a degree course, but some idea of the reality of the professional world outside.

Students are given early experience of working intensively on group projects, portfolio management and exchanging self-, peer- and tutor-assessment. The principle of the shared reviewing of progress and planning the next stages is built into tutorial dialogue and the more formal assessment points. The foundation course gives students both the opportunity to choose their own future specialism and the feedback on performance to help them do it.

Foundation course students are introduced to the art and design tradition of public demonstrations of achievements. Final assessment, even on a Foundation Course, includes the students' ability to select appropriate material and present it to external specialists and the wider community.

All students are required to mount an individual show of selected work. This is assessed, both by internal and external assessors, and a polytechnic certificate awarded accordingly, confirming the satisfactory completion of a foundation year. Great importance is attached to the presentation and hanging of the exhibition... The exhibition itself is widely publicized, especially to all schools over the wide area from which we draw our intake. {81}

One student's experience {135} illustrates the value of foundation courses in helping students explore their interests and decide the direction of their subsequent polytechnic studies. Andrea had access to a range of specialisms, enabling her to broaden her awareness of what was available and her own interests and abilities.

We spent time in all areas of design (photography, ceramics, graphics, fashion, textiles, etc). Initially I thought I would specialize in ceramics but... I came across weaving completely by accident. It was an area that I discovered for myself. I began by weaving paper, experimenting with different textures, colours and weaves, creating new effects. This I found to be extremely exciting.

At the end of her foundation course, Andrea was clear about what she wanted and was experienced in taking responsibility for her own development.

Admission by negotiation and students' work

By the time students are ready to apply for their HE course via the Art and Design Admissions Registry Scheme, most have a clear idea of what they want and where they can get it. It is not unusual for students to take the lead in exploring the facilities and ethos of likely programmes – often by day visits and discussions with tutors and students – before submitting a formal application.

On their part, admission tutors admit students on the basis of their portfolios of their work, their ability to assess their own work and their articulation of their longer term professional intentions. Capability potential is as important as prior academic achievement, as this admissions tutor explained {40}:

What we are looking for is their potential creative ability, objective criticism and understanding of their own work, and evidence of a clear sense of direction and commitment.

A typical admissions procedure would involve a whole day. Activities include: group discussions with staff about the course, facilities and diverse learning/career opportunities, formal tests of basic skills and general knowledge; and individual interviews to give students the opportunity to talk about their portfolio of work, to explain their reasons for applying and to discuss how they intend to use the course to further their longer term aspirations. Final year students are often included in the discussion of applicants' suitability. All current student year groups are involved in the giving of information to prospective students during open day visits prior to application.

Induction into responsibility
Despite the foundation courses and the admissions procedure, art and design programmes do not assume that their students have the capacity to act independently at the outset. The exposure of students to a range of activities, concepts and basic skills continues throughout the first year curriculum. Mastery of basic skills is considered to be of prime importance, not only to help students make realistic choices but also to help them perform well in a professional capacity.

Short intensive workshop programmes are provided in most key skill areas, often built around group projects. Once inducted into the basics, students are expected to continue to develop their skills through subsequent activities. Students learn the procedures for accessing studio and workshop facilities, including the benefits of help from studio technicians. The technicians, in fact, are a crucial element in the whole skills support service, providing individual advice and expertise whenever specialist studios and workshops are open for students. Students, in turn, learn how to make use of technical support for their creative activities.

In effect, the whole of the first stage of art and design courses, including formal assessment points, is devoted to continuing the process of helping students make informed choices about their professional future based on mutual assessments of their skills and interests. In one polytechnic {80}, for instance, the first assessment point is significantly called the 'gateway assessment', clearly signalling its role in the continuing development of the student. Progress is reviewed in the light of tested skills, interests and aspirations and the future direction for the student is agreed with the student. The programme leading to the gateway assessment is:

> ...designed to cover the basic experiences which it is felt the student must have in order to be able to make an informed choice of pathway.

As a consequence, student decisions about the future are negotiated with the benefit of evidence of the student's skills and interests in a range of contexts.

> After satisfactory completion of the gateway assessment, students individually discuss with the gateway assessment panel their appropriate pathway through the final two years, and arrive at a mutually acceptable choice.

In summary, the art and design experience shows how the early stages of higher education programmes can be geared towards giving students the basis on which they can build their own distinctive programmes of study. The whole course infrastructure, from recruitment priorities and procedures to resource allocations and assessments, supports the development of student capability. It has shown that giving students a grounding in a range of basic skills is not incompatible with students taking responsibility for their own learning. Indeed, the skills make it possible for students to take advantage of that responsibility.

Theme Two: Planning, negotiation and approval

Most art and design students are expected and encouraged to participate in all decisions concerning their studies. Student negotiation of programmes is part of the culture; approvals of plans are informal and flexible. In most cases, students and tutors share responsibility for the decisions which emerge. Not many courses – final year formally assessed assignments (see Theme Four) being an exception – provide for the formal approval or validation of learning contracts. Continuous critical dialogue enables staff and students to shape the overall coherence of the student's experience, from admissions to completion. Tutorial exchanges are less about the giving of information or formal instruction than about discussing the development of the student's work, and what might be done next.

The introduction of modular structures makes it more difficult to sustain this continuity and informality. To accommodate transient participants, individual modules on art and design courses have predetermined explicit objectives and learning outcomes for all students, thus limiting the extent to which the 'all through' art and design student's total programme can grow out of the experience of the student. One consequence of the modular approach is to make the process of negotiation and approval more explicit and formal. Students are required to enter one such course {234} by formally 'negotiating briefs' at the outset of their second year. This particular programme recognizes 'that each individual will have his or her own interests, skills and competences' and sets out to provide opportunities for the development of these within the overall context of the area of study, but imposes explicit requirements which all students must meet. For instance, in putting together a team for their group project, students must demonstrate they can:

- clearly identify aims and objectives;
- anticipate the skills/competences/knowledge required to attain the aims and objectives;
- assess fellow students as to their suitability/willingness/competence/ability to function adequately in their required roles;
- assess their own abilities/knowledge/suitability to carry out certain functions and enlist help where necessary;
- anticipate and allocate realistic workloads; and
- schedule the production.

In this scheme {234}, student plans are approved if, after discussions with staff, they are seen to be appropriate in terms of:

...realistic aims and objectives, anticipated duration, budgetary requirements, and learning outcomes.

The above example illustrates how, even within a structured, modular programme, student responsibility can be assured. The explicit programme requirements – the criteria against which all students must be judged – relate to process issues (objective-setting), the development of personal skills (self- and peer-assessment), and the demonstration of competences relevant to the industry the students hope to join (budget control, deadlines, team-building). The specific objectives of the students' work are a matter for the students themselves. One concern about the less formal sharing of responsibility for the decisions which emerges from critical dialogues is that the general criteria used by the staff in advising students may not be explicit. Decisions emerge because they 'seem right' in the light of the students' experiences and intentions. What constitutes good or desirable practice may be understood by the participants, but is not always spelled out.

Negotiation is not an easy option for students. The obligation to be open about their choices demands rigour. Deciding one's programme is daunting because one's whole professional future is at stake – and it is down to the students to justify their choice on the basis of their proven competence and commitment. Decision making, even in the less formal learning environments, is taken seriously as Andrea recalls {135}.

By the second year I had to make a decision and specialize in one area. It was a hard choice between print and weave because I had enjoyed and been successful in both areas. Although I could have specialized in both, I opted to concentrate on weave as it was a specific skill to learn.

Theme Three: Active and interactive learning

With the exception of some history of art components, the learning environments for most art and design students are the studio, the work-shop, the community and the work-place. The variety of individual interests, the demands of industry, the nature of the discipline and the emphasis on student responsibility do not easily accommodate delivery modes of teaching. Active and interactive learning are therefore the norm. Three widely practised activities are explored in this section: team-working; live projects; and placements and residences.

Team-working

Team-working is a feature of most art and design courses. There are two main reasons why this is so. First, team-working reflects the nature of the business itself, where many different specialists have to collaborate to convert ideas into reality. Second, team-working is a way in which students can pursue different specialisms while maintaining contact with the wider range of related activities. Students can share expertise and learn from each other. On one such course {134}, for instance, team-work is seen as:

> central to the production of media in terms of students taking on particular roles within a production team, working together as a team, and producing a quality product.

Team-working, in other words, is not a fad of the methodology of teaching; it is a legitimate part of the student's professional development. It is also used explicitly to give the student experience of 'discharging responsibility to him/herself and simultaneously to the group'. Teams are not confined to students. They frequently include technicians, tutors and external clients working in partnership. They often work within the discipline of externally imposed criteria of success.

Experience of collaborative projects helps students become less de-pendent on their tutors and be more self-reliant and supportive of other students. Staff have found that a reduction in their contact with their students, confined to key process activities, has the effect of helping students become more responsible and accountable for their own learning, as this tutor reports {133}.

> Self- and group-managed learning is implicit in the structure of such collaborative subjects. Curricular and tutorial time is maintained at a minimum throughout the exercise and is concentrated at the nodal points of briefings, interim critiques and presentations. We have found that a reduction of academic staff contact during the project has helped to create greater personal accountability within the peer groups.

Moreover, experience of working together without constant supervision by their tutors also raises student confidence in their own ability to explain to their colleagues and clients what their work is about.

> The overall project structure helps students in gaining confidence in the presentation and justification of their concepts to a critical audience of peers, tutors and senior management; a communication skill vital to success and effectiveness in their ultimate professional roles in industry. {133}

Tutors also report that self-directed team-working has a beneficial effect on the students' capacity to judge the performance of themselves and their colleagues. Team projects are strongly product driven, not tutor driven, so students need to develop clear product specifications to plan their work. Product specifications enable students to judge: (1) the capacity of each member to complete the work, (2) the actions they need take to fill gaps in their abilities, and (3) the extent to which they have been successful.

> In undertaking group projects students are required to carry out assessments of potential in regard to themselves and other group members. Can I or X carry out adequately the requirements of the set task? If not how can this be overcome? Equally, on completion, how well were each individual's, and their own, responsibilities carried out? Importantly, were their initial assessments at the beginning of the project accurate and realistic? It is this feedback through which students are required to test their own and others' judgement which is of great value. {234}

In summary, team-working is an essential part of art and design education because it is the essence of the design industry; it widens students' experiences of different skills, it develops key personal skills of communication and evaluation, and enables tutors to concentrate on the students' overall professional development.

Live projects

One of the main vehicles for the development of student capability on art and design courses, and one of its most distinctive features, is the 'live project'. A live project is an assignment negotiated by students and/or their tutors with clients working within the students' intended or potential professional field. They are often three-way associations, involving the tutors as professional practitioners, as well as the clients and the students.

Live projects can be commissioned by outside organizations or can be initiated by the college itself. The staff of the Visual and Performing Arts Department at Newcastle upon Tyne Polytechnic {134}, for instance, saw an opportunity for a live project in an initiative being sponsored by the local police.

> The Northumbria Police, who had collected over 800 weapons during a firearm amnesty,were looking for ways in which this might be used to good effect. We decided to put this to the students as a second year project in which they would prepare drawings and maquettes for a sculpture based on the theme 'Swords into Ploughshares'.

This particular live project illustrates another feature of art and design courses: the use of competitions to emulate the reality of the fierce competition within the business itself. Winning can be prestigious. In the case of the police project, the presentation was made by the Home Secretary. For the successful student, the design of the sculpture was not the end of the matter. Excellence had to be demonstrated in both the design, manufacture and the delivery of the product.

> At every stage of the process the student was involved in the planning, organizing, the written presentation, the submission for the exhibition and the planning application, and attended the meetings and made presentations to the planning committee, negotiated with the City Council on the installation, negotiated with the foundry, and worked with the Police Authority and the commissioners. She was involved in the organization of the presentation with the Chinese community in the area where the sculpture was erected, with representatives of the various religious faiths in the city who dedicated the sculpture at the unveiling ceremony, and with the Chief Constable and Sheriff of Tyne and Wear, and the Lord Mayor. {134}

Live projects enable students to gain an insight into aspects of their business not normally accessible within the confines of the college. They enable students to learn what is involved in dealing with actual or potential clients. In the case of the Newcastle gun sculpture, the success-ful student gained experience of working with four different groups outside the college: the body commissioning the work, the groups producing the sculpture, the formal bodies whose approvals were needed, and the community within which it was to be placed.

Where ready-made live projects like 'Swords into Ploughshares' do not exist, staff may have to go out and negotiate them for their students. This requires staff to be in close touch with trends in the professional world outside the college and to have the credibility to enter into realistic negotiations with hard-pressed employers. The resultant projects can be a genuine collaboration between the college and the client, matching the students' development and the client's needs:

> The subject matter would be mutually agreed and a typical time-scale of five or six weeks would involve a site visit to the manufacturing plant coupled with an initial project briefing by management staff. Course staff would then provide the studio tuition, general management of the project and prepare the students for an interim presentation of design concepts to the 'client' after approximately two weeks. {208}

The benefits students derive from live projects are not confined to experiencing the commercial reality of their intended specialist field. The quality of the studies also benefits, as staff on one course report.

> When students are involved with 'live' projects and real deadlines, we have found that the quality of work they produce and their performance improve dramatically... We believe that the student emerges from these 'real work' experiences better equipped to assess and deal with the challenges of professional life in his or her future career, particularly where the project has involved analysing available data, negotiating and describing a design solution, and then completion of the task to the client's satisfaction... {208}

According to the above experience, the live project work contributes to the quality of students' work through: (1) the discipline of deadlines, (2) the sharing of information and expertise through collaboration with staff and peers, and (3) the obligation on students to be explicit about their work to critical external professionals.

An alternative to the negotiated contract with outside companies is the purpose-built replica of the commercial world within the college. One polytechnic {232} provides an in-house design studio to:

...expand on the experiences provided within the normal academic environment. It enables the student to use and develop their communication skills with face-to-face meetings with a real client. The completed design work is presented at the commissioning company. A price is obtained from the printer. The artwork is produced. The student is involved in establishing the criteria for assessment and in the assessment itself. It is an excellent example of how to provide a total academic and commercial experience for advanced design students.

Staff also benefit from working with students in the design studio {233}:

> The work creates the necessity for staff to discuss and assess new teaching and learning methods, develops a more critical attitude to the learning processes and assessment criteria, and provides staff with the opportunity to update their own professional and commercial experience.

Live projects present college staff with a constant opportunity to monitor the relevance of the course to external circumstances, and to evaluate its effectiveness. They provide opportunity for genuine partnership between the industry and the course, giving each a valuable insight into the other. They enable students to meet practising designers in a commercial environment while also providing an insight into the latest commercial practices and equipment. Representatives from the design industry have the opportunity to contribute to the education of young designers and to influence course development.

Placements

Placements give art and design students an extended opportunity to absorb the milieu of the design business and to develop the skills which will enable them to survive within it. Art and design placements are seen as being much more than 'a year in industry'. They are seen by tutors, students and employers as integral parts of the students' programmes. The students do more than experience the industry; they explicitly learn from their experience of the industry. Employers take their educational responsibilities for their placement students very seriously; they see them as young professionals and they are potential employees. They use them on front-line work.

Frequently, the college and the employer collaborate on helping students develop their personal capability as well as their specific competence, as this joint feedback form illustrates {135}.

Please comment on the student's:

> *Motivation*
> *Communication skills*
> *Attitude to work*
> *Ability to assimilate and collate information*
> *Decision making*
> *Ability to work in a team*
> *Potential leadership*

The employers' view of what constitutes capability is indicated by comments they choose to make when giving feedback on individual student performance. For motivation, for instance, good student performance prompted the following comments from employers:

- a consistent self-starter;
- self-motivated... got on with it... asked for help when needed;
- self-motivated – did not require constant supervision; and
- easily motivated – once briefed was able to complete projects on her own. {135}

Employers such as Wallis Fashions {228} vouch for the effectiveness of these partnerships in developing the all-round capability of students by their willingness to employ the students afterwards.

> Students from the fashion marketing course use their wide-ranging skills and abilities on their placement with us. We benefit from the practical and innovative ideas students bring to the company and this balance of qualities also makes them attractive potential employees. {228}

Because tutors and employers put great emphasis on the educational value of the industrial placement – and are seen to be collaborating to make them effective – students also take the experience seriously. Students see the industrial placement as an essential part of their own professional development and seek to get the best out of it. They want a good company, specializing in their own field, and offering relevant learning opportunities. Students choose their placements accordingly, as reported by Julie {228}.

> When choosing my first placement I took into consideration: (1) the type of company I would like to work for and (2) how my design philosophy would fit into that company.

Julie was not disappointed with her choice. The company gave her the kind of experiences she needed and wanted.

> After I had chosen Wallis I was told what the placement entailed. It was exactly what I was looking for: to spend half of my time designing a coat, to produce the pattern, toile and finished garment – in cashmere; then to go through each individual department, with constant guidance from their outer-wear designer; also to spend the other half of my time in various departments – such as the press office, production and quality control; to learn how each department operates and liaises with each other; and finally to help out with general duties in the pattern room... to do a very wide and thorough placement. {228}

Not only has Julie learned a great deal, she has also enjoyed the experience and is eager to learn more.

> I have been doing all of this and find it thoroughly enjoyable. So far it has been a valuable learning experience, especially knowing that there is still plenty to do and learn. {228}

Another student, Andrea {228}, reports how much she appreciated being given serious things to do. She saw the placement as 'part of the course', not an interlude away from college.

> The year spent on industrial placement was a very valuable part of the course... I was designing fabrics that were put into production, made into garments and sold in the museum shop... the year gave me a lot of understanding about the weaving process and its commerciality. {228}

The company's officer with responsibility for supervising Julie and Andrea's placements explicitly sets out to ensure that students placed with her company gain experiences which supplement the skills gained in the college. She recognizes the importance of students actually wanting to make full use of the placement for themselves.

> These girls are very intelligent but because the colleges they attended did not offer courses with depth to encourage their capability, they made the decision to work in a fashions company to expand their knowledge. {228}

Students greatly appreciate the educational value of their placements. A group of students on a fashion course {135} readily reported to us what they had learnt about the industry from their placements and the skills they had developed. Most developed greater commitment to the industry and confidence in their ability. They particularly liked being taken seriously, being used as professional practitioners, and having access to all aspects of the business. This compilation of student comments summarizes their general view of placements:

> My placement gave me a much clearer understanding of the commercial fashion industry. I learnt the importance of communication with staff and with buyers, how to work as a team, how to visualize somebody else's ideas and cost-effective sample cutting. It gave me the confidence to deal with various clients, from company directors through to customers on the shop floor. The placement was a great confidence booster. I was able to see how a design evolves from inspiration to sales and was allowed to work with all levels of the company. We learnt how to be professional.
>   They gave me experience of incorporating my own design skill with those of the company's and I was invited to get involved in a whole multitude of new experiences. Due to the absence of the clothing manager I was often required to make decisions fairly quickly on a highly responsible basis. Overall it was an excellent experience and will have a great influence on my future work. {135}

The close relationship between the industrial placement and the college components of the course – and the art and design tradition of helping students plan their own professional development – enable students to follow up their placement experience with further voluntary association with the employer and, more significantly, into the post-placement college programme and the students' final assessments. Placements, in other words, can be used to involve employers more directly in students' final year programmes and final assessments as well as give the students' final year programme and assessment a firm grounding in the professional area.

Fine art students have less opportunity than fashion and design students to engage in live projects or extended placements with professional organizations. A different tradition, 'artists in residence', has emerged. Such schemes bring art students into contact with the wider community where they often find themselves questioning the relevance of their studies both to themselves and to others. On one such scheme {42}:

> ...all second year students undertake a four- to six-week artist in residence project within a public context outside the college. Here they spend approximately half their time working as an artist with the host community,

and the rest on development of their personal practice... The residency experience is a mandatory component of the second year, linking both with studio concerns and the contextual studies component, through which it is currently assessed.

One criticism students make of the scheme is that they often fail to get the opportunity to carry on with their own work during the placement. They get drawn into helping in other ways. The residency scheme, however, offers a vehicle for the development of capability, giving students experience of negotiation and the management of time and resources.

This is an experience largely self-managed by the student, who will discuss the project with the co-ordinator and then, jointly with her, negotiate the details with the host concerned. {42}

Regular college-based seminars provide an opportunity for reflection on the residency experiences, the development of presentational skills, and collaboration.

The weekly seminars, whereby students return to college contact, provide a forum for exchange of experience, discussions of approach, and presentation of work achieved, as well as contextualizing the experience through a variety of investigations – historical, theoretical, current case studies, etc. This provides a framework fostering the residency, and peer-group support plays a dominant role here. {42}

The benefits of the residency scheme are illustrated by the experiences of one student painter who was placed in a local school. The experience improved his understanding of his own work, and of the relevance of art to life in general.

I have found the residency very beneficial to the way I think about art and, consequently, my work. I have found that some of the things that (school) students do highlight the problems with my own work... often their mistakes are the same as mine only they are harder to spot in me... I have thought a lot more about why we make art as a result of thinking about a strategy for teaching. {42}

Theme Four: Assessment
The formal assessment of art and design students presents particular problems. The expressed aim of most art and design courses is to

encourage students to develop their distinctive professional identity, and to demonstrate it in live and often external contexts. The more successful courses are in achieving this aim, the more difficult it is to use standardized assessments. The challenge is to find forms of assessment which allow maximum individuality in the specifics of a student's work, while placing equal professional and intellectual demands on all students seeking awards of a similar level.

The variety of forms of assessment used is considerable, including exhibitions, designs, working models, cat-walk fashion shows and portfolios of drawings. What they have in common is the use of panels of assessors, direct presentations by students to critical and informed academic and professional audiences and prolonged viva-voce examinations. Student exhibitions are often supported by critical reviews of their own work which, in turn, are scrutinized by external academics and professionals. The rigour of this approach is impressive. As one student reported:

> ...other students just take written exams. They don't have to hang their answers on the wall for all to see. {134}

Two contrasting examples are now examined in depth.

The Newcastle upon Tyne Fine Art Degree {134}. This is a typical example of the all-through integrated programme. Its formal assessments, conducted at three different stages in the programme, show how some of the above issues are tackled.

First, the regulations explicitly acknowledge the problem they are designed to address:

> Clearly in a course which encourages self-motivated exploration, the emphasis in assessment must take account of highly individual programmes which may indeed re-define subject areas within the totality of fine art. {134}

Second, the three stages of assessment explicitly allow students to progress through the course from foundation skills and knowledge into individual development. Third, the regulations emphasize general criteria against which student performance can be judged, thus allowing space for individual specialist aims and objectives to be pursued.

First stage assessment, for instance, is concerned with the 'assimilation of basic techniques'. Criteria relate to the student's:

- aptitude in the use of methods and materials;
- comprehension of the basic elements of artistic expression;
- capacity to command fundamental critical concepts in fine art; and
- understanding of the history of the visual arts. {134}

The second stage assessment explicitly allows for student individuality to develop. The regulations are quite categoric in this respect:

> ...the student's progression is measured in terms of growing personal identification with a particular range of attitudes and media. {134}

The criteria for the assessment of the student's 'work in progress' relate to the student's:

- exploration and enquiry rather than finished product;
- critical self-scrutiny;
- intellectual apprehension of the creative process; and
- engagement with historical and critical factors. {134}

The second stage assessments are organized by the students themselves, and 'no stipulation is given concerning the work a student should choose to include', except that they will be judged by the above criteria.

By the third and final Stage, students are expected to:

> ...demonstrate the results of profound personal engagement with the intellectual concerns and techniques associated with their chosen practice. {134}

Criteria in this final stage relate to the student's 'commitment' and the programme's 'intensity'. Students must show:

- that personal research and critical reflection have been directed towards arguing a coherent case in their final project;
- breadth and depth; and
- awareness of modes of thought, practices and disciplines other than those of the main study. {134}

The assessments of student performance extend throughout the final term of the final year. Internal and external panels review student progress at the outset of the assessment cycle; they are able to see the work progress and engage in 'critical dialogue' with the students at predetermined points. This intensive use of examiners' time – in contrast with more traditional methods – is mitigated by the extent to which students have access to technician support and, by that stage, are not expected to be dependent on close tutoring. Significantly, the assessment task is shared with people from industry, which also ensures close scrutiny of the relevance of the students' work to the needs of the industry.

The rigour of the above assessments is clear. In addition to producing their specialist work, students have to articulate the basis for their assessment – including the specific criteria – and account for their achievements to internal and external panels of examiners, potential employers and, in some cases, the wider public. They need to be proficient in oral and written communication, setting their own objectives, self-evaluation, managing their own time and resources and in negotiation skills. They are also required to demonstrate a high level of independence in the context of their professional field.

The Leeds Polytechnic BA Honours Graphic Design Degree Programme {87}. This is a modular scheme. The Leeds scheme illustrates one way of ensuring that the commitment to the development of individually focused programmes can be preserved within a formal modular structure. The critical factor illustrated in the Leeds approach, visible also in the Newcastle fine art degree, is the clear separation of general programme requirements and criteria from the specialist objectives and criteria negotiated by the student. Students prepare and submit the brief for their proposed project or assignment for approval. The pro forma for the project brief requires students to spell out the specific aspects of the work, through which they will meet the general criteria for the course. In effect, they are required to negotiate the basis of their own assessment. The headings on the form are:

- Nature and context of work;
- Outline of brief;
- Objectives, specifications of work required and assessment criteria; and
- Reference material or research required. {87}

Students are given the criteria against which the proposed work will be marked before they begin the planning of their work. They are able to take into account the general criteria when negotiating their own specific objectives and criteria. The programme's criteria fall into three categories: personal development (eg, creativity, generation of ideas); educational development (eg, methodology, research, problem analysis); and vocational development (eg, application of media skills, appropriateness of final product). Other factors which are taken into account, such as commitment and attendance, are also made explicit.

The significance of the separation of general course criteria from the specific student objectives and criteria – whether in the all-through or modular programmes – is that it requires students to show how their own educational development and achievements relate to the level of the qualification they seek. The separation converts assessment into a valuable learning activity in its own right; it is challenging, develops and tests key skills and qualities, leads to a high sense of ownership and motivation, and promotes depth of understanding.

Issues arising from the art and design experience

The art and design experience provides strong support for the Education for Capability argument that giving students opportunities to be responsible and accountable for their own learning improves both its relevance and quality. High completion and employment rates, together with an international reputation for the excellence of many of its graduates, are achieved without the use of tightly controlled, predetermined knowledge-based teaching. The design business is very competitive; companies demand a high degree of commitment and professionalism from their recruits in order to flourish within it. Their belief in the quality of the distinctive approach of art and design education is shown by their willingness to play a full part in its central activities and to compete for its products.

To some extent the nature of art and design itself contributes to capability. Creativity and visual intelligence are important personal qualities. However, by directly involving students in the development of their own programmes and the justification of their achievements, other important attributes and skills are developed. These include confidence in their abilities, independence, commitment, critical awareness, communication skills, team-working, evaluation skills and decision-making ability. The use of client-based live projects as a central feature of undergraduate programmes requires students to address the needs of their own professional development in the context of the needs of the industry.

The most distinctive feature of art and design education, from a capability perspective, is the strong emphasis on student accountability at every stage, from initial interview, through the 'ongoing critical dialogue' style of tutoring, to final assessment. The examples quoted show how this key activity stimulates personal development, greater understanding and intellectual and professional rigour.

Art and design education shows it is possible to ensure that essential skills and knowledge can be covered within a structure dedicated to the independent development of each student. Close links with the external professional environment, at every stage, make students aware that high levels of technical competence are essential ingredients of personal development. It is their commitment to their own personal professional development which motivates students to work on their basic skills; it is their basic skills which make their professional development possible.

Other disciplines have similar features to art and design (where the application of skills and knowledge is as important as their acquisition) but have developed different educational cultures. A major factor determining art and design's distinctive approach to learning is that it has not grown out of the traditional university approach of the acquisition of knowledge for its own sake. Art and design education as it is known today developed from the aftermath of the Great Exhibition in 1851 where the dismal standard of British manufacture had aroused considerable disapproval both from Government and royalty. As a result the Department of Science and Art established a number of art schools which, after a Royal Commission in 1886, became schools of art and design. These had the specific aim of relating arts, craft and design to industry and manufacture through a process of practical and technical education.

There is no overall professional body controlling entry into employment. Control resides in the direct working links between industry and the college, and the mutual concern for the students' proven professionalism.

There is a tradition of employing staff, either full- or part-time, on the strength of their professional experience and links with the industry. Many practise their professionalism, and demonstrate their commitment to becoming better at it, alongside their students, blurring the distinction between consultancy, staff development and teaching. Close working relationships with industry ensure effective collaboration over student placements.

The availability of technicians to give specialist advice on technical matters means that students can become independent of academic staff, with consequential benefit according to some of the evidence. Tutors can be available for 'critical dialogue' about the idea, the strategy and the outcome of the activity and about each student's progress. In one polytechnic department, there is one technician to every two teaching staff.

The concerns about the modularization of courses and resource constraints focus on key capability features of the art and design tradition – skills support, individual development, tutorial styles and close professional links. The examples illustrate ways in which modules can retain some capability features; the effects of continuing resource constraints on part-time staff, technical support and tutorial styles may not be so easily mitigated.

Chapter Four
Capability Through Business and Management

Susan Weil and Philip Frame

Forces for Change

This introduction highlights external and internal factors which are influencing and supporting the way in which business and management programmes in higher education (HE) are developing. These include:

- the debate about British management and business education, stimulated by various major reviews (see for example: Constable and McCormick, 1987; MCI, 1990; Handy et al, 1988; and Training Agency, 1989);
- changing interpretations of the manager's role;
- developments in our understanding of learning processes; and
- various initiatives that are raising issues about learning processes and outcomes generally in HE, including Enterprise in Higher Education, Higher Education for Capability and BTEC/SCOTVEC.

Business and management studies are concerned with relevance and performance effectiveness. The developments outlined above focus attention not just on the 'what' of learning but also on the 'how'.

British management and business education

As Constable and McCormick (1987, p. 6) recognize, 'One of the most important resources possessed by the nation is its managerial skills.' Yet, 'to the British management it has always been more of a practical art than an applied science' (Handy et al, 1988, p. 7). Nevertheless, business and management education has become an established subject of study in British higher education.

As perceived initially by Franks (1963), the purpose of management education should be to improve the effectiveness and capability of managers in whatever environment they operate. But, what constitutes management effectiveness and capability and, in turn, what kinds of academic knowledge, processes and assessment strategies will foster its development?

The manager's role
Since the early 1970s, studies have attempted to define the characteristics of effective management but, as Bennett (1984) has demonstrated, there is no uniform definition. Such studies emphasize, though, the importance of developing not only knowledge and awareness, but also understanding and capability in both the 'hard' functions, such as marketing and finance, and the 'soft' functions, such as leadership, communication and decision making.

In addition there is growing awareness that managers must continue learning during their working life and help others in the organization to do the same. Thus, how they learn and the development of this capability is becoming as significant as what they learn. Indeed, the former could be regarded as one 'constant' of working life when compared to the increasingly transitory nature of knowledge.

The process of learning
Research has also raised issues about the utility of what might be termed 'the conventional classroom approach to learning' with its disproportionate emphasis on the student's ability to acquire and record knowledge.

Considerable debate within management and business education has focused on the role of action (Revans, 1971) and more recently experiential learning (Kolb, 1984; Weil and McGill, 1989). Recent research into 'deep' rather than 'surface' learning (Marton et al, 1984; Ramsden, 1988; CNAA, 1990–ongoing) and adults as learners (Knowles, 1986) is also having an impact by focusing attention on the role of the tutor, the learning needs of the individual and the importance of students taking greater responsibility for their own learning, individually and in groups (Prideaux and Ford, 1988). Indeed, there is growing recognition that the quality of learning can be enhanced by giving students the opportunity and motivation to apply their knowledge. Mintzberg (1990) is quite explicit: 'We are taught a skill through practice plus feedback, whether in a real or simulated situation.'

Other forces for change
Government agencies are also raising questions about what and how we teach, and how we can best help others learn. The Council for National

Academic Awards (CNAA, 1984) and Her Majesty's Inspectorate (HMI, 1989) have supported the inclusion of skills acquisition and participative learning methods in higher education courses.

The work of the Business and Technical Education Council (BTEC) and the Scottish Vocational Education Council (SCOTVEC) is exerting an ever greater influence on the prior experience and expectations of students by emphasizing the value of activity-based learning, greater employer involvement and learning to learn.

Equally, the Partnership Awards and Enterprise in Higher Education (EHE) have helped to stimulate and recognize innovation. The latter in particular has complemented the Higher Education for Capability's emphasis on active and interactive learning and on students assuming more responsibility and accountability for their own learning.

The Management Charter Initiative

Recently, radical changes to the learning process in business and management education have been proposed, including the concept of a Management Charter Initiative (MCI). These proposals (Handy et al, 1988) are part of a trend towards competence- and outcome-based approaches to education as evidenced in the work of the National Council for Vocational Qualifications (NCVQ) (Jessup, 1991) and the Universities Council for Adult and Continuing Education (UCACE) Learning Outcomes Project (UDACE, 1991).

Perhaps the most controversial aspect of the MCI has been the adoption of what might be termed a 'standards' approach in the definition of competence. This initiative is arousing considerable debate in management and business education about, for example, the concept of a national list of competences, whether competence development can or should be the focus of higher education and how competence should be examined/assessed.

The debate

The debate about competence as opposed to a broader notion of capability will continue. A Manifesto for Management Development has now been launched as a counterpoint to MCI. The thrust of the counter-arguments is that a broader and longer term approach to business and management education – more akin to that advocated by the RSA HEfC initiative – is required. MCI critics point to factors such as the sheer pace of change, equal opportunities, developments in Europe and the complex realities managers face in their roles.

The key issue is whether participants should work to a prescribed set of narrowly defined competences, or themselves be involved in the continuous formulation and re-formulation of criteria by which their performance is judged, especially in different kinds of organizational and cultural contexts. The latter places emphasis on the continuing learning and development of managers and their capability to be responsible and accountable for managing that process (Burgoyne, 1989; Cunningham, 1991).

Conclusion

The management and business education debate is not being conducted in a vacuum. It is occurring in the context of very significant developments in the form and process of learning in higher education generally and in the light of changing demands from the turbulent environment within which the sector operates. Higher Education for Capability offers much of value to such current debates. Academics and their clients need to be aware of how the sector is responding to the general thrust of the campaign, and why.

The examples that follow illustrate some of these responses. They aim to contribute to the vitality and direction of continuing debate and to encourage further developments that will enhance the quality of management and business education.

Theme One: Reviewing and building on experience

Students of management and business studies bring to their studies life experience of being managed by parents, teachers, policies and procedures. More students have been and are in part-time employment. What do they know about managing people from being managed?

Encouraging the utilization of past and current experience provides an effective starting point for learning. Conceptual understanding is enhanced, is more powerful and longer lasting when students can relate pertinent theory and principles to their experience.

The examples submitted placed little emphasis on drawing on students' prior experience. Those that did were largely post-experience courses. In contrast, undergraduate courses focused on creating current and ongoing learning experiences on which further learning could build.

EXAMPLE 1: Learning from teamwork – the first year experience

At Middlesex Business School, 97 first year students on the BA Business Studies degree {125}, a four-year sandwich course, participated in a pilot workshop programme associated with the EHE initiative. Students worked in small teams with both a task and a process focus to their activities. The aim was to provide students with a different perspective on, and experience of, learning that would serve them well as managers in future. The student group was divided into 17 small teams of five or six members. No criteria were used in selecting members for each team.

Task focus: Each team generated a business idea and produced a business plan. These included: a home shopping service, a post-school nursery and a management training course. This year's activities involved the skills of applying financial, production, personnel and marketing knowledge to the development of the team's business ideas.

Process focus: Teams met fortnightly for a staff-supervised three hour activity-based workshop, guided by explicit aims and objectives. Formal knowledge inputs about roles in groups and teamwork were provided.

The results of each group's activity were presented for assessment both in writing and orally. (See below under Theme Four: Assessmsnt for some details.)

Philosophy and practice of learning
This initiative was based on a view of undergraduate education which, in the words of the tutor:

> ...begins to put learning/the learner rather than teaching/the lecturer at the centre of our activities. We wanted students to begin to reflect on the 'how' as well as the 'what' of learning {125}.

Learning is often taken for granted as having a single meaning. Research, in fact, disproves this notion. Experiential activities designed to encourage students to reflect on their learning in different contexts help them appreciate the complexities of learning processes. In this case formal inputs were provided on:

> ...learning, including the social aspects of learning, different modes of learning, the use of experience and the setting of learning objectives. In subsequent workshops, they were required to put theory into practice. {125}

Preparing students for a process focus

It is sometimes assumed that by putting students to work in teams, they will automatically learn from their experience. Rather, research shows that reflection on such experience, assisted by conceptual models, is essential if learning is to take place.

> The most important aspect of the programme, and one that is sometimes overlooked in group-based work, concerned the process whereby groups become teams and how each team operates to solve problems: that is, the team process. {125}

In this case, support for this way of working was provided through:

- formal inputs;
- accountability criteria (ie, for teams to analyse the team's process); and
- informal tutor-led (and latterly student-led) process consultation within individual teams. {125}

The identification and improvement of communication skills was also an explicit aim of this programme. Communication can be improved through experience, practice and feedback, but learning will be enhanced by conceptual input and reflection opportunities:

> In this case formal inputs, including videos, were provided on both making presentations and non-verbal communications. {125}

Changes

The success of programmes such as this is dependent on changes to features normally 'taken for granted', including: the role of the student and student groups, the role of the lecturer, and the physical environment.

Students

This programme placed different, and often unfamiliar, expectations on students.

> They needed to become more active in their learning, and be less passive and dependent on lecturing staff. Because of the team-based nature of the programme, they were encouraged to participate and interact with their peers, academic staff and visitors from the outside world. This was not an easy change to make. {125}

An evaluation of this programme revealed that a number of students had not worked in this way previously and were intimidated by the prospect.

- Learning in a group – with and from other people – has been a new experience for all of us.
- At first I was absolutely terrified, nervous and apprehensive. I could not bring myself to say anything and neither could anyone else. {125}

The tutor asserts that:

> These feelings, though, can be present in lectures, seminars or tutorials. Emphases on active learning and on process provide opportunities which help overcome such anxieties; a passive approach to learning only reinforces them. {125}

Learning about the advantages and disadvantages of teamwork, and strategies to overcome the difficulties, was one of the most frequently identified benefits of the programme:

> I believe any lessons we may have learnt will be remembered for longer than anything learnt in a more traditional way. {125}

Lecturers' roles
Lecturers had to become less the 'fount of all knowledge' and more facilitators of learning. They also had to engage in a more complex set of activities, including:

> ...working as a team, exerting influence rather than control, explaining and justifying the form and content of the programme, engaging in discussion and debate, dealing with here and now issues, being a process consultant and accepting feedback. {125}

Physical environment

> For students to work in teams they need an environment which facilitated this, that is, tables and chairs to accommodate a team of up to six people and for as many teams as are meeting for a particular workshop. Currently, all our large rooms are arranged for formal lectures. {125}

Conclusion
The social dimension of learning: The affiliation needs of students, now well documented in research, and especially that on drop-out of mature

students in the mass HE system of North America , are all too often met only through out-of-class activity. This can leave overseas, part-time and mature students with a sense of isolation that can undermine their motivation and engagement with a programme. As an overseas student commented:

> The most successful part of the workshops has been the teamwork. When people who have never seen each other before and come from different backgrounds and cultures have to work closely together in a group, it causes each individual to develop a more balanced and broad outlook. {125}

The social dimension of learning – when made an explicit and valued academic concern – should not be underestimated when considering the overall quality of student experience.

New dimensions to quality evaluation: These students were exposed to different experiences and meanings of learning than found traditionally in HE programmes. This programme provides a different reference point from which to determine what counts as quality and raises issues about the paradigms within which appraisal of professional performance, student evaluation, quality ratings and resource decisions are located.

EXAMPLE 2: Experienced-based development of management competences

At Teesside Business School a compulsory module of the Certificate in Management Studies – Managing Self in a Social Context {215} – enables participants to define their skill and learning needs in relation to their current employment and their aspirations for advanced study. Participants are part-time students, mostly in their first management posts, with an average age of 30.

Learners generate profiles of themselves. They diagnose their present levels of management capability through undertaking a variety of enquiry procedures designed to promote self-evaluation. For example, they are required to provide details of their background, engage in self-evaluation, identify measurable goals, specify how these will be achieved and indicate their success criteria. The outcome of these processes is a personal-development plan related to the capabilities they see as necessary for their satisfactory performance in employment. These plans are implemented at work.

Participants make oral and visual presentations of their self analyses and personal programmes in the context of peer-group review and aid the group in agreeing capability levels relevant to a variety of management activities. Throughout the module, they are accountable for communicating and reporting on the outcome of their plan, indicating further development needs and how they intend to meet them. The emphasis is thus on self-critical and continuing appraisal of personal development needs in the context of employment.

This module was introduced for the benefit of students who were returning to higher education, or who were uncertain of their career development. It has now been incorporated into the CNAA validated Certificate in Management.

Assessment is by portfolio, incorporating a personal-development plan, the students own support-learning agenda, an evaluation of outcomes of diagnostic materials, and evaluation of peer-group reviews. There is no unseen time-constrained examination of the module.

New skills for tutors

The role of tutors on this programme is more as participant than provider; more mentor than teacher. Tutors need to:

> ...inculcate in participants a frank awareness of personal strengths and weakness through the formal study of the nature of human activity systems and capability development. {215}

This course is based firmly on developmental principles but tutors need to ensure that the end of this module is not the end of the developmental process because 'one of its aims is to produce a life-planning approach to personal capability in employment' {215}.

The emphasis on continuous development and self-appraisal requires lecturers themselves to demonstrate a capacity for critical reflection on their own performance.

> Relatively few teachers possess the ability to inspire participants to question what material needs to be learnt, what skills developed and why. Negotiation towards personal development requires teachers to be comfortable in human relations, confident in academic discussion, knowledgeable about a wide range of work-places, and good communicators. {215}

Tutors are also challenged to develop new ways to manage academic learning structures and processes which are responsive 'to the practical requirements of employment, in the context of the capabilities of the individual' {215}.

Discovering the validity of an alternative approach
The impetus for this module grew out of

> ...a number of competence-based developments within the school. In
> addition, individual staff members attended seminars and a national con-
> ference on the subject of skills, competence and capability. {215}

In this example the individual's development plan becomes an integral
part of the curriculum. Aimed at returning post-experience students, it
was intended to be an intellectual exercise as well as a practical exploration of individual goals and intentions. The major obstacles were:

> ...attitudes towards a relatively high proportion of skills to knowledge
> compared with past programmes and the need for a lower staff/student ratio.
> The first has been overcome primarily by staff development and employer
> pressure for greater efficiency and the second by exploring different
> methods of curriculum delivery. {215}

What counts as academic knowledge is a growing debate. Skills learning
and the technical application of knowledge has traditionally been regarded as of lower status in the academic world. In some arenas, even
education and business degrees themselves are suspect bodies of knowledge. Although the module counts for one quarter of the final assessment, it has been found that it:

> ...plays a far more important part in overall course activity than is suggested
> by this figure. It sets the scene for many other activities and the development
> of a wide range of skills, all geared to agreed capability levels in keeping
> with the MCI initiative. At the same time, although students know what to
> expect from the programme, they can also influence and add to the com-
> petences that are staff generated or MCI influenced. {215}

Staff confidence from increased experience of working in alternative
ways has created the motivation to extend this approach to a wide range
of management programmes from first to senior levels.

> We are in the first year of running a modular management development
> programme of a highly integrated nature in which personal-development
> planning will form a major initial component.{215}

Resource implications
Implementation of this module has required the allocation of:

...time and other resources to classroom presentations, general discussions, remedial guidance of participants and structured peer-group review sessions. {215}

The major resource implication has been:

...staff time in liaison with participants at their work-places for the purpose of eliciting job-performance information. {215}

Also, with this approach:

...time for small group and one-to-one discussion is necessary, even though typical tuition within the School operates normally at a much higher group size. In terms of group presentations and personal assessment sessions, some expenditure is necessary for audio-visual equipment. {215}

Conclusion
Though more resource intensive than a conventional approach, an approach which focuses on learners' experience and interests has been shown to work effectively and is providing the impetus and example for further change. The value and validity of this alternative approach to management development became somewhat clearer when lecturers actually became involved in working actively with participants. Many of those involved have begun to realize that:

...students should be involved in setting the goals of their own capability acquisition. It is resource intensive, though not excessively so, but requires a more fundamental change in attitude towards teaching and learning on the part of all participants.{215}

Theme Two: Planning, negotiating and approval
Challenging students to take more responsibility for their learning, to learn how to set goals and critically review their performance, is particularly pertinent to the development of managers. Managers are obliged to be responsible for others. At the very least, therefore, participants must learn to take responsibility for themselves.

As managers they will be appraising others' performances. Again, they need opportunities to do the same with their own performance. Managers also have to find ways of meeting their own continuous development needs within their organizations: a balance between individual goals and those of the company will always be a subject for negotiation. It is therefore appropriate that experience of such negotiations be an integral part of their education and that there is scope for contracts to involve their own managers, mentors or company representatives.

The use of learning agreements and active student participation in negotiating learning aims and outcomes are generally found on post-experience courses. This is likely to change, as BTEC shapes the expectations of entrants to HE. For example, all BTEC students must now keep a profile of their competency achievements.

EXAMPLE 1: A university validated MBA by self-managed learning
At Roffey Park Institute, a two-year part-time executive MBA programme validated by the University of Sussex {163} was introduced in January 1990. The entire course is based on the principles of learner responsibility and accountability. Participants thus manage their own learning and assessment, individually and collectively. There are six key elements in this self-managed learning programme:

(1) the philosophy of self-managed learning (SML);
(2) the learning contract;
(3) mapping the field;
(4) the set;
(5) the assessment process; and
(6) the tutorial support {163}.

The philosophy of self-managed learning
This programme is rooted in core values about the process of managing.

- Managing is an active process. Managers need to be able to demonstrate that they can manage.
- Managers are required to make sophisticated and difficult judgements... Therefore, it is appropriate that they submit their judgements to the scrutiny of peers as part of the management development process.
- Managers should manage their own learning if they are also to manage others. {163}

The learning contract
SML is a process by which managers devise their own programmes of work and study. The learning contract provides the means whereby rigour can be maintained.

It is the mechanism which ensures that managers *do* set learning goals/targets. To help them in this process, managers are commonly asked to think through given questions. {163}

For example:

- Where have I been? Where am I now?
  Outcomes: Clarification of learning needs.
- Where do I want to go? What skills do I need?
  Outcomes: definition of goals.
- How do I get these?
  Outcomes: initial formulation of plan of action.
- How will I know if I have arrived?
  Outcomes: Initial formulation of basis for assessment. {163}

The learning contract is, however, a two-way process. Managers are expected to agree their learning goals, firstly with their support group (or set) and secondly with their organization. As such, SML represents a very concrete way of tying management development directly into organizational strategy, which would appear to be a growing concern in organizations today.

The learning contract is also about getting learners to think about the process of learning itself.

By encouraging a manger to think through not just *what*, but also *how*, he/she might learn, individuals think back to past learning experiences, both positive and negative, and what that says about the sorts of approaches to learning which appear to work for them. {163}

This initial learning contract is not fixed. Participants are able to re-negotiate their contracts over time. Evaluation research does show, however, that perceptions of negotiation can vary considerably and can be seen by some participants as an 'admission of failure or a miscalculation.' The 'blank slate' approach can also be criticized heavily, on valid managerial grounds. Thus one participant pointed out that, far from operating with a 'blank piece of paper', managers invariably face barriers to learning because of their organizational settings. Such barriers should be acknowledged in the initial contract, thereby reflecting the realities of organizational life.

Mapping the field
The last point above leads to the need to help learners to make choices. On the MBA the first seven months is both a time to write a learning contract and a time when course participants are given a chance to see how experts define management. At the end of seven months they not only have to produce a learning contract but also an essay of up to 20,000 words analysing their own perspective on the field of management. Further, they are encouraged to find a mentor in their organization so that a bridge is maintained into the organization's needs and direction.

The set
The set provides another accountability framework, and a challenge to critics who see self-managed learning as merely self-indulgent or lacking in rigour. As in many action-based learning programmes:

> ...individuals are formed into groups (of five) for the purpose of offering support, feedback and the benefit of their experience. {163}

For most, the experience of sets tends to be very positive and powerful:

- I think its very useful having people who I can actually be totally honest with.
- It was very personally stressful but beneficial – I had one or two intense periods of time which were very painful but I knew I was learning. It was done in such a way that I found very constructive... it was done primarily through the sets but also through the set advisers. {163}

This last point underlines the reality that there is little significant learning without pain. This raises issues for student evaluations of teaching and learning. Critical or mistimed feedback could lead to learner responsibility and accountability being rejected, or becoming instrumental and little more than an exercise in collusion. Only by ensuring that these processes are genuinely rooted in dialogue and in an appropriate balance of challenge and support can HE assist in the rigorous development of the person and intellect.

Assessment
The learning contract, including the objectives agreed originally and re-negotiated over time, provide the basis for a collaborative assessment process.

> Anyone managing their own learning should be able to judge their own work... However, these self-evaluations need to be checked with others, and so the course requires that the individual's peers (the set) form a crucial 'check and balance' on the personal judgement. {163}

Additionally, employers, external examiners and the set adviser are involved in the process, which can, therefore, be far more rigorous than traditional methods. Although peer-led, the process can nevertheless result in student failure.

> By adding the set adviser's judgement, the useful 'expert view' of a traditional assessment process has an equal voice and the decision on a pass or fail has to be reached by consensus. {163}

Where consensus is impossible, external examiners are more directly involved.

Tutorial support

A key person in the process of tutorial support is the set adviser. Possible roles, which can be the subject of negotiation, include:

- *Ordinary set member* – giving information and ideas;
- *Catalyst* – doing something that no-one else is doing, such as confronting issues that no-one else is prepared to;
- *Process consultant* – helping with the process by which things are done, such as conflict resolution or effectiveness reviews;
- *Link person* – acting as a contact with other interested parties such as employers; and
- *Adviser* – identifying resources, and ground rules that course members have to abide by. {163}

Evaluation

Evaluation research is currently being carried out on the first graduates.

EXAMPLE 2: Contracting for on-the-job and off-the-job learning.

At Durham University Business School, a one-year postgraduate Diploma in Enterprise Management {36} is offered to students of any discipline. The course begins with a two-week residential introduction to management, based on experiential learning approaches. Participants are then matched with a company where they are employed on a full-time permanent basis. Students are responsible and accountable for their own learning via the following.

(1) On-the-job learning

- A learning contract must be negotiated at the beginning of each term between the student, the employer and the student's academic mentor.
- A series of three projects has to be agreed between the three parties involved. One of these forms the basis of a dissertation. {36}

(2) Off-the-job learning

- Monthly workshops (two to three days) which deal both with functional and personal competence development are set up. The precise content of the workshops is negotiated between the group and the course director.
- A learning support group is established. It operates both outside and inside the formal workshop sessions, incorporating elements of peer-group appraisal. {163}

Candidates are assessed throughout the year and also by two formal seen examinations, one of which is a case study. The employer is also involved in assessing the extent to which the student has met his/her learning objectives.

Ensuring rigour
Each student is placed in a small or medium-sized enterprise to provide realistic experience of management. This enables them to learn how taking responsibility and being self-reliant increases their confidence to take action and make decisions.

The course is designed to ensure that placements enhance the academic quality of the learning experience. Students are accountable not only for the development of functional and interpersonal competences, but also for ensuring that this is actively linked to a sound understanding of relevant theory.

The emphasis on responsibility ensures that the learner is continually obliged to make meaningful connections between practice and theory, in ways that are conducive to deep, rather than surface, learning and to more effective performance.

Resistances and extensions
When introduced, this course's explicit emphasis on a holistic understanding of management and on creativity, communication, competence

and co-operation provoked scepticism. This came equally from academics, employers and sponsors.

> These resistances were overcome largely by obtaining funding from the European Social Fund, and securing the approval of both the Board of Studies in Business Management and the Senate of the University... This in turn attracted public sector sponsorship, employer contribution and student registrations. Throughout, however, the provision of adequate and appropriate staff resources has been a problem, often having to be overcome by engaging tutors and mentors from outside the Business School. {36}

Now, with a culture shift:

> ...staff were prepared for their role as mentors through induction programmes. There is also a programme steering committee to provide advice and guidance. {36}

The culture shift is due largely to there being more emphasis on negotiating, contracting and student responsibility within university courses. Staff and employers have also benefited, as has the school and the institution.

> The course facilitates links with local small and medium-sized enterprises in the region and demonstrates the contribution which higher education can make to company performance.

> For the employer, the course provides an additional resource which enables projects to be undertaken which might otherwise not have been completed. Similarly it extends the company's network of business contacts to include higher education and breaks down any barriers which might have existed as a result of their perception and prejudices. Finally, it helps convince employers of the benefits of graduate recruitment and gives them an entrance to higher education. The Local Authority sponsors benefit by retaining intellectual capital in the region and through the development of the small and medium-sized enterprise sector of the local economy... {36}

Student and employer feedback
Information aimed at reducing resistance was secured through continual monitoring, including assessment by an external evaluator from the European Community who had a particular interest in employer and regional benefits. Employers have made the following comments:

- Universal has used Tony's [a student] enthusiasm and the support of Durham University's Business School to provide us with a major step forward in quality enhancement and product design. *(David West, Universal Transformers)*
- Tony, who has an archaeology degree, has breathed young life into aspects of our business and given us a different perspective. *(Bill Heaney, Bill Heaney Ltd)*
- Jim, who did an accountancy degree, has fitted in very well. The course has provided considerable benefit to him and so to us. Jim is now a part of our small management team – we need him. *(Peter Bell, Mailcom)* {36}

The benefits to students have been monitored via the Board of Examiners which includes moderation by an external assessor:

Apart from gaining competence in, and an understanding of, management, most students have gained in confidence and developed as individuals, often being offered employment on completion of the course. {36}

More specifically:

- The support network has been brilliant. A monthly visit to DUBS does much to restore your self-esteem and determination. Having done a pure arts degree, the course provided me with an excellent bridge. *(Sara MacLeod, BA Joint Honours, Harrison Brothers Ltd)*
- My last job was with a large multinational company and I felt I was just a number – someone to be forgotten about. Here I am much more involved and have a lot more responsibility. *(Keith Thompson, BSc Mec Eng, NICE Ltd.)* {36}

Conclusion

Whereas students and employers are perhaps more forthcoming about the benefits, this course still represents an interesting departure from normal academic practice. The weight of tradition and the status given to pure theoretical knowledge rather than to its application, remain more difficult obstacles to overcome. Resource cut-backs pose further challenges:

The main factors likely to influence the further development of programmes based on student responsibility are a change of attitude within higher education (many remain unconvinced of the benefits of such an approach) and additional resources to enable staff to develop the programme to its, and their, full potential. {36}

Theme Three: Active and interactive learning

Active and interactive learning opportunities help students relate learning the real business of being managers to more formal material. While the use of projects is increasing, they do not guarantee quality learning processes and outcomes. They can in fact become an exercise in doing what is necessary to pass. Students can also experience projects as though in a vacuum, bearing no relationship to what has been learnt in other parts of a course.

Experience and action do not in themselves guarantee learning. We learn through doing and through reflection on doing. To be effective, students need guidance and time to reflect on active and interactive learning outcomes. Such learning will benefit from recurring dialogues about the coherence, the meaning and the interrelatedness of capability-based course components to the whole of students' educational experience. The following examples, while not addressing all of these concerns, aim to stimulate further debate and development.

EXAMPLE 1: Off-site learning – the power of the real

At Middlesex Polytechnic, company-based problem solving provides the major task focus for the second year of a two-year Enterprise Workshop programme {126}. Using off-site and company premises, small teams of students (five to six) are presented with a real organizational problem. Approximately 20 companies provide the context within which teams are accountable for collecting data on the issues and making an oral and written presentation on the results of their efforts, including recommendations for action, to company personnel.

Staff take responsibility for negotiating entry into the organizations, which include Osram, Manpower and the London Borough of Barnet. An outline of the problem to be addressed is agreed in advance. These are of genuine concern to the organizations involved. The dates of teams' first and final visits to their specific organizations are also finalized by lecturing staff. Within these parameters, students are free to manage the exercise as they see fit. The autumn term preparation entails a focus on organizations and change: why change, what to change and how to change. In addition to a formal knowledge input, students attend a programme of three-hour workshops in which they work in teams on tasks which encourage them to apply that knowledge. At the same time, they focus on the team process and oral presentations. (Additional preparation comes through a first year programme described under Theme One: Reviewing and building on experience.)

Assessed tasks include a written report to the organization and an oral presentation to company representatives. Company representatives were involved in the assessment of oral reports produced for their organizations and in the provision of feedback to the teams on their performances.

The meaning of off-site learning

In this example, off-site does not refer to any arena in which learning takes place, but rather to:

> ...a predetermined and specified location – an organization – which is unconnected with and geographically separate from the usual environment in which students experience teaching and learning, in this case the Business School. {126}

Learning in situations that really matter to those involved – to clients and students alike – can be extremely powerful. This factor was critical to the achievement of course objectives by students. The programme's intention is that, by its conclusion, students would, for example, have:

- clarified a real organizational problem;
- collected and analysed relevant data;
- utilized polytechnic-based learning;
- recommended appropriate courses of action;
- demonstrated that they could work as a team; and
- effectively presented themselves and their work. {126}

The power of the real

Feedback from students suggested that the objectives referred to above were achieved. This exercise was powerful for them because:

> ...it engaged their interest or motivated them; it was powerful because it was both challenging and enjoyable. Why should this be so? The significance of being in 'a real organization' or a 'real firm' was often referred to. As one student said: 'I think the first thing that actually got us interested in this was the fact that we were dealing with something serious that was actually relevant to someone and had some importance to an external organization.' {126}

The reality and power of the learning exercise was further enhanced by virtue of the fact that students had contact at managerial level.

While most students have worked in organizations, few have had any contact with senior personnel. The level of their contact, and the expertise and experience these post-holders were perceived to possess, were seen to add a degree of credibility and importance to what the teams were doing. {126}

People not students

As importantly, students were struck by the treatment they encountered in their interactions with their organizations.

- We were treated as people, as consultants; it made us feel really good.
- Everyone treated us with respect and as adults not as students.
- We were not introduced as students but as people who may be able to help them. {126}

For young students, who made up the majority on this programme, this was a critical factor in their development. Equally, they recognized their own responsibilities in managing the reality with which they were presented.

For this task we had to change ourselves from students to professionals and to adopt a professional style, ie, be systematic, be well prepared and work effectively as a team.

It is essential that the client takes you seriously. This means, for example, dressing smartly, appearing confident, and interested, and knowing what you are talking about. {126}

Being involved in a real organization also helped to underline for students the significance of theory in relation to practice. According to one student: 'This experience gave me the first indication that a knowledge of management theory did actually have a place in reality' {126}. Indeed, experience of organizational reality helped one student to learn 'never to dismiss something as mere theory' {126}. The course tutor remarks: 'It would appear that reality as defined here supports rather than undermines knowledge of theory' {126}.

Gains for employers

The problems participating organizations identified included:

- how to respond to radical environmental change;
- how to improve the induction of new staff; and
- how to facilitate interdepartmental communications. {126}

Industrial partners indicated that the outcomes of this pilot programme were significant:

- The students got interesting feedback for us which we couldn't have got ourselves. Lots of things they said we were aware of, but they formalized and defined ideas for us. They forced us to take action. *(Training Manager)*
- Last year's group was very good. They changed our perceptions of why staff come and go. As a result, we changed our recruitment focus and turnover has been reduced. *(Personnel Manager)* {126}

Conclusions

Risk taking: This programme was introduced with the ostensible aim of providing opportunities for student learning through closer collaboration with other organizations. In the context of this Business School, this off-site, small team-working was unusual for undergraduate students:

> Our experience has led us to conclude that it was worth taking the risk...
> We as lecturers must be alive to the fact that the nature of the tasks we set have a profound impact on the degree to which we encourage or discourage learning. One way to encourage learning is to engage students with real life. We need to expose and exchange other methods which will perform the same function. {126}

Learner self-esteem: An unanticipated outcome of this exercise was that students' self-esteem was significantly bolstered. The extent to which students commented about 'being treated as people, as adults' suggests that this was a relatively new experience and gives rise to the question about whether or not lecturers' attitudes to students encourage a sense of self-worth and, if they do, how. {126}

EXAMPLE 2: The strategic use of case studies to develop student capability.

At Sheffield City Polytechnic, the BA (Hons) in Accounting and Management Control {173} includes a final year option in Financial Decision Making. Here the development of personal skills and qualities is integrated into a course that is entirely case study and group based. The case studies are chosen to examine problem situations of a broad business nature. They are multi-disciplinary and encourage problem identification as well as problem solving. Students work in different groups for each case. Role play and structured tasks foster the integration of subject knowledge, personal skills and creative thinking processes.

The case studies derive from the experience of staff. Increasingly, partnerships with industry, commerce and the accounting profession give rise to jointly developed materials which also meet the training needs of the organizations concerned.

Case studies are approached by using a standard three-step procedure for each one:

(1)   A briefing session where the case is distributed, the requirements outlined and students are allocated to groups.
(2)   A session where the case is run, whether by role playing or presentations.
(3)   A debriefing session where students are encouraged to analyse their potential solutions and their experience.

This procedure takes approximately two weeks. During this time, students are responsible for convening informal meetings to develop their work.

This course developed in response to the demand of accountancy firms, who required more than technical skills from graduate recruits. In 1990 it won the 'Group Skills in Accountancy Partnership Award' provided by Coopers Lybrand Deloitte Chartered Accountants. The subject will become core in 1992/3.

Developing academic, personal and subject specific skills simultaneously
The objectives of this group-centred learning programme are identified as:

(1) *Personal skills and qualities*

Students should have identified and developed:
•   the ability to work within a group and the communication skills this involves;
•   the negotiation skills necessary in identifying and analysing a problem and proposing solutions within a group;
•   the need within a group to allocate tasks and motivate others;
•   recognition and acceptance of leadership qualities and skills;
•   intra- or inter-group presentation skills; and
•   the ability to question assumptions, listen to arguments and respond accordingly.

(2) *Academic skills*

Students should be able to:
- identify the particular subject skills and knowledge appropriate to a particular problem;
- appreciate the difficulties involved in clearly defining problem areas;
- apply and integrate previously acquired subject skills and knowledge; and
- evaluate, classify and organize information into a suitable format for the application of decision-making techniques. {173}

The explicit aim is therefore to use learning strategies which encourage skills development that go well beyond the traditional taxonomy of academic skills:

> These learning methods must be sufficiently adaptable to encourage students to enter into 'live' discussions, debates and arguments about very real business issues. {173}

The nature of tutor involvement has been carefully thought through, based on experience over a number of years.

> The learning methods are monitored by at least one tutor being in attendance whenever the students meet to present their opinions, choices or views about a particular case. If the participants see an issue quickly and resolve it, then the cases used are sufficiently adaptable to introduce new variables which are pre-planned by the tutoring staff and which it has been suggested may, or may not, arise in the case scenario. {173}

Monitoring and evaluation: the need for a more responsive approach
In this situation, continual monitoring and review is central to the culture of this course, and is seen by tutors as a core responsibility:

> This process establishes an interactive cycle of monitoring which means case material, presentation and group process are reviewed and amended if necessary. {173}

The course is also subject to internal monitoring procedures as prescribed within the polytechnic, including staff/student consultative committees for each year of the course. However, these can prove inadequate to more student-centred ways of working:

Tutors believe that this particular process has too long a lead time for this style of course and that the monitoring of learning processes and methods is best done by adopting the interactive process described above. {173}

Conclusion
Developing student responsibility and accountability is not limited to case study work within this institution. This traditional vehicle, used in an innovative way, enhanced knowledge, improved skills and confidence, thereby providing a way to develop capability.

Theme Four: Assessment

Introduction
As a consequence of our growing understanding of what promotes effective performance, either as learner or as manager, far greater emphasis is now placed on individuals and small groups being responsible and accountable for subjecting their own performance to continual review and monitoring. This is increasingly being reflected in HE assessment strategies, some of which now draw on far more sources of information and involve others in addition to the subject tutor, including self, peers and employers. Journals, portfolios, projects and oral presentations are all vehicles for development and assessment. Assessment is thus becoming more multidimensional in terms of what is assessed, how it is done, who is involved and for what purpose.

The examples that follow represent attempts to grapple with such issues by introducing new thinking and practice.

EXAMPLE 1: Group-based peer-assessment.
At Middlesex Polytechnic, group-based peer-assessment was introduced to the second year Enterprise Workshop Programme of the BA Business Studies {127}. Students worked in small teams on organization-based problem solving. Peer-assessment was introduced in the context of learner-centred teaching strategies and a commitment to less traditional modes of assessment. It was clearly geared to promoting learner responsibility and accountability.

To heighten consistency between course objectives and modes of assessment, the course team sought to send complementary rather than conflicting messages through the assessment process. Student input into the assessment provided a means for them to exert some control of the process, while exercising creativity and responsibility.

It was made clear from the outset that individuals were, as members of a working team:

> ...accountable for their actions to that team. At the same time, it (peer-assessment) gave teams a potential control mechanism in respect of individual members and the authority to use it.
>
> Assessment overall is based on individual effort and team output. The former category counts for 50 per cent and includes a case analysis, an account of individual learning and peer-assessment. The other 50 per cent comprises an oral and written presentation and a review of team process. Peer-assessment counts for 10 per cent of the individual's final mark. {127}

Procedures for this assessment process are set out in the course handbook and are introduced at the beginning of the academic year. The written parameters are as follows:

> • Firstly, each team should devise a set of criteria which indicate the sort of behaviours which tend to help or hinder the teams' activities. Your criteria may include creativity, task performance, attendance, etc. It is for each team to decide.
> • Secondly, each member should be assessed in relation to these agreed criteria and be awarded a mark out of ten by the other members of the team, with a higher mark being awarded for more effective behaviour.
> • Thirdly, these marks should be clearly noted in your report, together with the team's justification for each member's mark. {127}

Thus, the lecturers did not impose a set of criteria, recognizing that:

> ...while there may be certain risks associated with this strategy, we believed that the benefits derived from ownership of the criteria were of greater significance. Additionally students had to provide a justification of the awarded mark. It was thus more than a numeric exercise. {127}

The course team also recognized that such processes are largely unfamiliar to students, and preparation and support (both formal and informal) are vital. For example:

> ...they were provided with inputs on teamwork, peer-assessment and giving feedback; they were given the opportunity to utilize this information in activity-based workshops and were themselves given feedback by staff on their team's activities. {127}

Outcomes

This approach proved to be anything but mechanistic or instrumental for students. Rather, it was developmental and educational in a number of unexpected ways:

> All but one group followed the instructions... and in most instances they went beyond their brief by, for example, outlining the process whereby they managed the exercise, and defining the categories in use. It was apparent that the task was taken very seriously indeed and that a degree of thought had gone into how the process could best be managed. {127}

Groups certainly did not find the challenge of sharing responsibility for assessment easy. They reported: 'We spent a long time doing peer-assessment – the session proved both painful and useful, but always constructive.' This seemed to stem from the reluctance to express negative evaluations. One way to overcome this was to sanction such expressions. For example, as one student reported: 'We agreed that the process should be constructive; there would be no hard feelings towards anyone who spoke their minds.' {127}

This approach emerged as part of an overall pattern of managing the complexities and of peer-assessment:

> It involved the anticipation of problems and dealing with these by setting ground rules to which everyone agreed. This was seen as a means of ensuring fairness and reducing potential conflict. The ground rules for most groups involved brainstorming a set of criteria, agreeing these, applying them to an individual while they were out of the room, agreeing a numerical score and a rationale for this, giving the individual the opportunity to comment on their assessment and reaching agreement as a team. {127}

The number and range of criteria used by the groups varied between eight and 23, with the majority of groups using between ten and 14. Some groups reported having identified larger numbers and then reducing them to a manageable size. With regard to marking:

> ...no-one scored below five or above nine. In the majority of groups, a range of two marks was used and in only two groups was a range of four marks used to differentiate between members. This suggests a possible reluctance to differentiate dramatically between team members. Alternatively , it may well reflect the reality of team performances. What these results do demonstrate is that students will neither award themselves top marks when they are given the the opportunity to do so nor will they use the opportunity to settle scores by giving very low marks. {127}

The responsible and analytical way that students approached the task is a common theme in reports of peer-assessment.

> It suggests that the fears of those who object to such involvement are based on a perception of students which is not reflected in practice. It might even go some way to undermining those fears. {127}

Tutor's role in peer-assessment
The tutor's role in such a process is inevitably going to be different and unfamiliar; it is specific and restricted.

> It involves ensuring that the criteria are met and, if they are, recording the mark awarded. This limited involvement is sometimes difficult to accept, especially when presented with work of varying quality. Any attempt to assess the quality of output must be resisted though. {127}

Repeatedly reported as the most difficult challenge is letting go of control:

> Having given the responsibility to the students, the tutor cannot then take it away. If this is done, the exercise could no longer be defined as peer-assessment. If we want to encourage responsibility in our students, we must provide them with opportunities to be responsible. {127}

Conclusion
The means by which tutors introduce and facilitate a rigorous approach to peer-assessment are critical: the legitimacy, the timing, the preparation, the instruction, and the support are crucial to success.

Tutor confidence in the validity and value of an alternative approach is essential. If the departmental culture discourages risk taking, pressures against alternative approaches to learning become strongest at the assessment stage. It is then that questions of quality are raised. This example shows how the quality of assessment experiences for students can be enhanced by giving them a degree of responsibility.

EXAMPLE 2: A portfolio approach to assessment
The BA (Hons) Public Relations at Leeds Polytechnic {88} was created with the objectives of Higher Education for Capability in mind. A core commitment to wedding theory and practice required the establishment of a Public Relations Studio, refurbished by sponsorship and the polytechnic.

Each student is adopted by one of 83 public relations companies or in-house departments. Self-generated project work, and the creation of a portfolio of achievement as the means of assessment, are key features of the programme.

The role of the portfolio

Courses which emphasize active learning and skills development for specific career paths can raise concerns within an academic environment. Will higher learning and understanding of theory and research be given a low priority, or indeed abandoned altogether? This was an obstacle that the course team set out to tackle, via specified objectives for the portfolio approach. These were:

- to give students the opportunity to put theory and learning into direct and meaningful practice;
- to encourage and recognize student achievement in applying public relations skills;
- to ensure that the full range of public relations skills have been acquired by the student prior to the conclusion of the degree programme; and
- to demonstrate to potential employers that the student has achieved fully professional working standards across a wide range of public relations activities.

The portfolio is assembled continuously throughout the degree programme, with new elements added and older elements upgraded at frequent intervals. Assessment follows normal professional criteria.

The most significant issues are whether its contents would be successful in normal commercial situations and whether the portfolio would fully persuade a potential employer of its creator's abilities. High standards of accuracy and presentation are vital. {88}

Students are required to exhibit and give formal presentations on their portfolios. The manner of these presentations is formally assessed. While examples of portfolio content are recommended, it is made clear to students that they are expected to find additional ways of demonstrating their creativity and initiative.

Illustrative contents – direct representation

Articles, reports and letters to editors An early first year portfolio might include word-processed articles, reports sent to newsletters and letters sent to editors. These would be replaced at a later stage by writings in their published form.

Media releases Copies of releases with distribution lists and evidence of any coverage gained.

Leaflets/brochures In their final printed form such items would be suitable; otherwise, the text, with plans for print, layout and illustrations.

Business presentations Slides and/or acetates with presentation notes.

Photographs/illustrations Samples of work; published versions would be particularly valuable.

Edited work One or more newsletters, magazines, journals or occasional publications edited or co-edited by the student.

Illustrative contents – indirect representation
In a number of cases there will be no immediate visual 'product' of public relations activity which can be placed in the portfolio, and the activity thus has to be represented in an indirect manner.

This will again test the student's initiative, but some indicative examples follow.

Market and opinion surveys Summaries of surveys, using graphic presentation.

Exhibitions Promotional posters, plan diagrams, photographs of the exhibition and results achieved.

Opportunities for students to produce any or some of the above may result from staff directed activities, such as events management; from staff introductions to clients; from student initiated activities, such as participating in clubs and societies or from the company who has 'adopted' an individual learner.

Conclusion
This example demonstrates the wide range of artefacts and events which can form the basis of effective capability assessment. It strongly suggests that we should look beyond traditional modes which focus on unseen, timed and non-collaborative assessments. Rather we should be creative and, as in this case, utilize the the type of activities and outputs that a professional would produce as a means of providing quality assessment.

Conclusion

The eight examples presented above provide a flavour of the type and range of innovations that are currently being made by colleagues in HE institutions. They demonstrate the ways in which the 'taken for granted' of teaching and learning is being effectively challenged in order to facilitate the acquisition of capability. In particular, the significance of collaboration, and of practices which are more in tune with the realities of life and work, are highlighted.

Academics are working in partnership with a number of their client groups to a greater extent than in the past. These clients include the learner, their peers, the learner's sponsor and other outside organizations. The focus of collaborative work includes:

- utilizing past and current experience, both in and out of class, to aid the process of learning;
- helping clients decide their learning objectives and aspirations;
- engaging clients in decisions about the process and sources of learning; and
- involving a variety of clients in assessing the outcomes of the learning processes.

Thus the nature of formally recognized learning relationships has become more complex. While their management demands a different use of resources, the results extend the degree of responsibility and accountability by involving all who have an interest in the learning process.

At the same time, the growing use of alternative sources of learning, and the focus on different ways of learning in HE courses, encourage the integration of what is taught and what is utilized both in work and in life generally. Courses which take account of the world outside HE institutions, of professional and organizational practice, demonstrate ways in which theory and practice can be strongly linked. In this way, learners are encouraged to recognize that they can continue developing over time, rather than restricting their opportunities to those provided on educational and training courses.

Acknowledgement

The introduction was prepared with the help of Prof. David Kirby, Durham University Business School.

References

Bennett, R. (1984) 'Management Education for Real.' In: Kakabadse, A. and Mukhi, S. (eds) *The Future of Management Education.* Aldershot: Gower.

Burgoyne, J. (1989) *Management Education and Development.* 20, 1, pp. 56–61.

CNAA (The Council for National Academic Awards) (1984) Personal Transferable Skills.

CNAA Improving Student Learning Project. (1990–ongoing) Oxford Centre for Staff Development.

Constable, J. and McCormick, R. (1987) *The Making of British Managers.* North Hants: British Institute of Managers.

Cunningham, I. 'Bridging the gap between academia and industry.' *The Guardian,* 11/2/91.

Franks, Rt Hon Lord (1963) *British Business Schools.* London: BIM.

Handy, C., Gordon, C., Gow, I. and Randlesome, C. (1988) *Making Managers.* London: Pitman.

HMI (Her Majesty's Inspectorate) (1989) *Quality in Higher Education*: A report on the HMI invitation conference at Heythrop Park.

Jessup, G. (1991) *Outcomes: NVQ's and the Emerging Model of Education and Training.* Lewes: Falmer Press.

Knowles, M. (1986) *Using Learning Contracts.* San Francisco: Jossey-Bass.

Kolb, D. A. (1984) *Experiential Learning: Experience as the Source of Learning and Development.* Englewood Cliffs, New Jersey: Prentice Hall.

Marton, F., Hounsell, D. and Entwistle, N. (1984) *The Experience of Learning.* Edinburgh: Scottish Academic Press.

MCI (1990) *Management Competences: The Standards Project.* Management Charter Initiative.

Mintzberg, H. (1990) 'The Manager's Job: Folklore and Fact.' *Harvard Business Review,* March/April, pp. 163–76.

Prideaux, S. and Ford, J. E. (1988) 'Management Development Competences: Teams, Learning Contracts and Work Experience Based Learning.' *Journal of Management Development,* 7, 3, pp. 13–22.

Ramsden, P. (1988) *Improving Learning: New Perspectives.* London: Kogan Page.

Revans, R. W. (1971) *Developing Effective Managers.* Newark: Appleton Century Crofts.

Training Agency (1989) *Management Challenge for the 1990s.* Sheffield: TA.

UDACE (1991) *What Can Graduates Do? A Consultative Document.* Leicester: Unit for the Development of Adult Continuing Education.

Weil, S. W. and McGill, I. (1989) *Making Sense of Experiential Learning.* Milton Keynes: SRHE/GU.

Chapter Five
Capability Through Engineering Higher Education

Susan Weil, Peter Lines and John Williams

Introduction

Finniston and beyond

Higher education has a vital role to play in developing capable engineers who can influence the advancement of the profession, the future of the economy and the quality of life in society generally. But just what does this challenge entail as we move towards the next century? And how are academic staff involved in engineering higher education responding?

Some ten years ago, the publication of the Finniston report (HMSO, 1980) led to the establishment of The Engineering Council. This set the standards and routes to registration for the profession. However, post-Finniston there are still many issues to be faced, including:

- what kinds of learning opportunities should HE be providing?
- just what will 'capable engineer' mean in future and how might such a person best be developed, given limited resources?
- how can the quality of engineering education be enhanced and indeed, what does quality mean in a move from an elite to a mass higher learning system?
- has the familiar approach of laboratories, lectures and tutorials in some cases become a treadmill and, if so, what alternatives are there and how can they best be introduced?
- are current ways of assessing students' abilities and potential as future engineers the best and, if not, what alternatives are there and how can they be introduced?

The need for capable engineers

High-level technical knowledge and skills are critical to the economic prosperity of the nation (HMSO, 1987). But is this enough?

A strong basis of specialist knowledge and the ability to apply it is essential to underpin effective engineering responses to new challenges and new markets. Today's engineers also need to be 'market conscious, commercially adept, environmentally sensitive and responsive to human needs' (Engineering Council, 1985). Employers want graduates who are flexibly and broadly educated, who can solve unfamiliar problems and can work in teams (Engineering Council & SCUE, 1988).

Engineers need to know how to make continual and effective use of work-place and educational resources to manage change and to update their specialist knowledge. This requires continuing education throughout their professional careers, the need for which has been recognized by the Engineering Council (1990). Greater emphasis on continuing professional development – stimulated by the rate at which technological knowledge becomes obsolete – must produce a re-appraisal of the role of the first degree in relation to continuing education.

HE is rising to these challenges in the initial education of engineers. The development of specialist knowledge is being underpinned by opportunities for students to participate in the development of criteria against which they can gauge their progress. More and more, students work through learning opportunities that simultaneously challenge them to take risks, make decisions, monitor their effectiveness as learners, be creative, and evaluate critically various solutions to unfamiliar problems. Such learning need not be at the expense of the acquisition of 'hard knowledge'; instead, an approach that entails responsibility and accountability can drive a far deeper conceptual and intellectual grasp of vital engineering principles and material (Sparkes, 1989, 1991; Hounsell et al, 1989).

The need for more engineers

Employers assert that there are insufficient engineers to meet national needs. The number of engineering graduates employed in industry has in fact increased by 50 per cent in less than ten years (Bonwitt, 1990). This change has come about at a time when the Government is urging a significant increase in the higher education age participation rate (HMSO, 1991). The demand for places on engineering courses among the declining 18-year-old cohort remains far too low (Smithers, 1990) although there are some signs that this trend is reversing (PCAS, 1991; Smithers, 1990). The recruitment of students with more varied academic, work and life experience becomes essential if the supply is to meet the demand.

In this context, current levels of dropping out and examination failure in engineering is of concern. It is in fact the, 'highest for all subjects both in the universities and in the polytechnics and colleges' and is now the subject of considerable research (Parry, 1990).

Structural solutions are commonly proposed. The staircase image predominates. 'Stepping on', 'stepping off' and 'pausing on the landing' are the kinds of metaphors that underpin arguments for modularity, the assessment of prior experiential learning, new interfaces between BTEC and A levels at school, and more engineering partnerships between FE and HE (Ball, 1989, 1991). It is also argued that public perceptions of engineering courses and careers need to change.

Creative and challenging courses that build effectively on the different starting points and aspirations of students, and equip them to respond effectively not just to the known but also to the unknown in the profession, are likely to prove more effective in attracting and retaining students (Macaulay, 1990).

Capability principles and practices as a way forward
The examples that follow in this chapter represent a wide range of interpretations of capability principles and practices. They illustrate the different ways in which academics are seeking to improve the quality and responsiveness of their programmes. They offer a variety of responses to the challenges of change, undertaken within the constraints and opportunities of their particular institutional or departmental situation.

Theme One: Reviewing and building on experience

Introduction: first year initiatives
Engineering faces particular challenges in setting a culture for first year studies. Students now vary substantially in their expectations of teaching, learning and assessment as well as in their background knowledge.

Most students are used to comparatively small classes and expect a formal setting. The first year must motivate students and this often implies a substantial content of engineering applications. Yet at the same time, the first year has to contain the necessary engineering fundamentals. Also, the first year carries the responsibility of developing students as independent learners, and as team-workers – concepts that can sit uneasily with students' previous experience and pre-conceptions of higher education. Yet if such expectations and culture are not established in the first year, it becomes progressively more difficult to establish it in subsequent years.

This section explores ways in which first year students can be introduced to some of the challenges that will later confront them in the profession they have chosen.

At Polytechnic South West, first year HND Civil Engineering students {195} are briefed to act in groups as junior members of a consultancy reporting to a 'Partner'. The intention is to use their innate curiosity as the starting point for grappling with initial principles of construction engineering and management. The consultancy activity has the following purposes:

- to increase awareness of construction procedures relevant to below-ground work;
- to foster self-awareness, imagination, creativity and interpersonal skills; and
- to enhance an individual's effective and efficient application of construction procedures.

Individually, and as a team, students submit staged reports on the feasibility of constructing a motorway – to the alignments and through the ground conditions indicated on an outline drawing. In doing so, they identify, research and report on construction problems, assess relevant construction procedures and propose/develop optimum solutions. This experience also provides a focus for reflecting on the benefits and problems of teamwork. At the end of the unit, students undertake an 'open book' style assessment.

Programmes such as these are often seen as competing with 'academic priorities' as defined strictly in content terms. This example shows that content and process need not be placed in opposition. When they are integrated, the quality of teaching and learning can improve significantly.

The approach adopted has freed time for the lecturer to concentrate on coverage of 'key' topics/issues. However, it has placed emphasis on the need to provide access to adequate, relevant reference material. {195}

As students gain more experience of taking responsibility, they also become more forthright in saying how they might better be prepared for a different approach. The following student feedback captures some of the above themes.

I think the first project should have been individual and easier with an obvious structure, amount of work needed, etc... For further projects, the students should be in groups of three maximum. This would allow for better/easier work distribution within the project, and make it easy for group meetings to do any work/reading which should always be done with group members around to allow for discussion, etc. Apart from these structural problems, the actual work involved in the projects was very relevant... I found the exam (open book) interesting to do and even enjoyable! {195}

At the University of Newcastle upon Tyne students at the beginning of their Engineering Foundation Year {138} participate in a module on 'Oral communications and teamwork'. This programme anticipates the development of students as future engineers in that:

- they experience working in groups of various sizes;
- responsibility is placed with the individual, but not at the expense of an emphasis on the learning community;
- students are helped to relate their current experience as students to situations they will confront as engineers; and
- emphasis is placed on the skill of giving feedback – a check-list is provided to facilitate peer-group assessment of individual presentations.

This programme places particular emphasis on oral presentations. One student writes with considerable self-awareness about this experience.

Giving a presentation can be an intimidating experience. You are laying yourself open to embarrassment in front of your peers, mockery, criticism and humiliation... In my experience, these feelings are the end of a long process of change in my perception of the ordeal to be faced. Initially, in relation to my title, I feel blank, and have the response, 'I can't think of anything.' This panic gradually subsides as I resign myself to the fact that it has to be done. Then, miraculously, I have a wonderful idea for a radical new approach which will dazzle everybody with my brilliance. This euphoria lasts for varying amounts of time – usually until I have finished writing, and then this too subsides and gives way to serious doubt.

This is the most dangerous phase since I start to change and rewrite my plan, often nearly beyond recognition...

Gradually, calm descends and the presentation is finally organized. Relaxed, cool, calm and collected I am eventually ready to give the presentation. Things do not stay this way, the inevitable last-minute panic seizes me seconds before it is my turn, but it is too late. I am committed to this version!

The first few sentences come out in a garbled haste, but then I am able to settle down and perhaps even enjoy giving the presentation. It is all over before I even knew it had begun – and the dominant feeling is a relief. My strong points as a presenter are a reasonable command of the English language and an ability to ad lib. An injection of humour or self-mockery can keep the audience alert and perhaps even interested. Once I am committed to the final draft and am standing in front of the audience I have quite a good degree of self-confidence and can project my voice well...

Presentations do become easier the more you practice but, in my experience, you never lose the last-minute panic. Once complacency sets in, a mediocre performance will ensue. As with most things, hard work pays off. The more time that has been spent preparing the presentation, the more familiar you are with it and the more confidence you have... This means you have more eye contact with the audience and this is important since giving a presentation is merely a formal manner of interpersonal communication. {138}

This student shows how her involvement has helped her to attend more explicitly to her competence and continuing development as a communicator – a quality that employers are now seeking in engineering graduates.

At the University of Hull, software engineering students {68} work in groups of four on a software system production exercise. Members of staff act as live clients and customers for the systems to be developed. Each member of staff is allocated a project, and remains the customer throughout its development. The student groups, however, change clients at the end of each of the four stages of requirements analysis; systems specification, design, implementation and testing.

From the students' point of view, they are responsible for achieving essentially two goals. The first, the ostensible goal of the exercise, is to take a vague system description and develop it into a well-defined, effective and feasible system specification, calling on theoretical and practical knowledge gained in a variety of courses taught in the first year. The specification is then developed into a design, implemented and tested. The second goal requires students to explore and learn effective ways of organizing themselves and the activities of the group. It is this second goal which provides the student with what we feel are the crucial challenges and opportunities. {68}

Employers were also involved in this programme, ensuring that the approach had relevance to industrial practice.

> We had very useful discussions on the relevance of the exercise generally
> to industrial practice with representatives of the Ford Motor Company who,
> incidentally, are presenting a prize to the best group effort... the exercise
> was designed so that the students would have to tackle these problems in
> the ways in which they would be tackled in industry. {68}

Experience at Hull suggests that the challenge to teachers and course
designers is:

> ...to ensure that the exercise results in the students acquiring skills and
> knowledge. It is a fact of life that students are more interested in building
> systems than in educating themselves... The most crucial factor to consider
> is the views and attitude of the staff who will be involved as clients as well
> as teachers.
>   There were a number of benefits to students, including the realization that
> working in a group requires communication skills and organizational effort.
> Technically, they learnt that the production of even an apparently 'simple'
> piece of software requires substantial effort at the requirements and design
> stage. Most groups, predictably given their level of experience, left a
> substantial proportion of design to the coding stage... One of the aims of
> the exercise was that it should help to equip the students with the communi-
> cation, co-operation and presentational skills likely to be of benefit to future
> employers. {68}

At Coventry Polytechnic, automotive engineering design and mechanical engineering students {28} share a common, traditional first year
course. In the second year the automotive engineering design students
move to a problem-oriented approach. Students are responsible for
solving the problems posed for them, drawing on their own knowledge,
experience and interests. This approach focuses their attention on the
skills they will need to improve their problem solving abilities.

The second and subsequent years are studio-based:

> ...where group work flourishes and a very useful by-product, peer teaching,
> has developed strongly. The automotive flavour of the problems set to
> students (for example, the design of a motor car cooling package including
> radiator, fan and water pump) has been found to be very motivating. {28}

The validation panel for the course included eminent representatives
from the automotive industry and staff from other faculties with oper-
ational experience of the proposed learning and assessment methods.
Validation was conditional on a staff development programme. A

strategy was developed, beginning with the course document as the basis for a training needs analysis. Members of the course team were encouraged to identify issues and concerns relating to unfamiliar aspects of the new curriculum.

Thus the staff development strategy itself adopted a problem-centred approach. In this way, a deeper sense of involvement and 'ownership' was fostered.

> The outcomes of the first day-long activity were used to plan a week-long intensive workshop-based programme. The general areas which were addressed included experiential approaches to learning, specifying learning outcomes, working in groups and assessment. A particular aim of the workshops was to enable participants to develop realistic project-based activities that would be appropriate...
>
> An evaluation... indicated that for the most part the aims of the programme were achieved and that the staff involved received it positively and enthusiastically.{28}

At the Polytechnic of East London {43} students have opportunities to enter engineering degrees through a foundation programme that is based entirely on the notions of student responsibility and accountability. This programme comprises four components:

(1) professional orientation and vocational guidance;
(2) core maths and science;
(3) new technology appreciation; and
(4) specialist study.

The programme content is student derived and managed. Students profile themselves, plan personal development paths and goals, and demonstrate their achievement through negotiated continuous and final assessment in a portfolio. Vocational guidance and counselling support is given. Subject support is given through workshops, tutorials, 'drop in' learning resource centres and some lectures.

Students may also choose to follow a recommended core content course covering prerequisite knowledge and skills required for all 26 undergraduate courses to which the programme is linked.

The 'professional orientation' component aims to develop the skills and understanding relevant to getting the most from a capability approach. They are helped to integrate these into their process of knowledge acquisition.

The first six weeks are spent in training and development in capability skills so that students have the tools to develop a 'capability' perspective in their studies and assessments, and take responsibility for achieving this. Skills developed include study, time management, organizing, decision making, communicating, interpersonal, leadership and team membership. Study methods include individual and group work, non-directed private study, practice at using resource-based learning, case studies, simulations and closed circuit television. Students design and negotiate a study contract. The final portfolio of work is assessed on the knowledge acquisition through laboratory, theory and practical studies. {43}

A capability approach requires teachers to have expertise not only in their subject area but also in the guidance and support of student learning.

Teachers have had to adopt new teaching strategies, integrating the monitoring of student progress and tutoring in capability with their subject expertise. They have developed communicating, negotiating and advocacy skills to support students' negotiations to join specialist departments. {43}

Time and space to make sense of the learning derived from new ways of working are essential:

Tutors spend considerable development time discussing the challenges 'educating for capability' has made to traditional learning conventions in science and engineering. They each developed sample study contracts in which excellence of knowledge acquisition and capability were integrally developed. This practice led to the rejection of study contracts in which subjects were conventionally sequenced, tutor paced, content determined and assessed in a standard format.{43}

Time release for course teams involved in ambitious capability initiatives such as this programme is an essential consideration.

The team members had time release to attend development meetings. These were run as workshops. A specialist tutor led the group for a specific component to develop overall aims and objectives. Sample study contracts were then developed for the component, demonstrating how capability skills and knowledge were complementary. {43}

An approach such as that adopted on this programme inevitably develops students who have gaps in certain knowledge bases, but considerable strengths in others.

Feedback from students who chose to transfer to universities from the first two cohorts indicates that whilst they might still require a broader knowledge base to compare with standard entrants, the quality of their knowledge and its application and their capability skills give them an advantage over their peers. {43}

Theme Two: Planning, negotiation and approval

Introduction

The development and negotiation of learning agreements with students is a fairly new innovation on engineering programmes. The examples that follow illustrate the different ways in which negotiating and contracting processes are being gradually introduced into engineering education, from open learning modules across a school of engineering, to the use of learning contracts and negotiated work programmes with a community partner – in this case a museum.

At Wolverhampton Polytechnic {243}, students have the option of contracting directly with an employer to receive credit for off-site work-based projects. A special module called 'learning contracts' was offered on a pilot basis to part-time and full-time undergraduate and postgraduate students in computer science, business information systems and information technology.

Developed with Training Agency funding, this programme enables students to complete part of their course through the negotiation of a contract between the polytechnic and a third party, normally the employer of the student. For example, two contracts were negotiated with Tarmac Quarry Products, both in the information systems area. They resulted in the production of software of a high calibre and the company is keen to use this method again.

Polytechnic tutors are timetabled for four hours of negotiation followed by 12 hours of tutorial support. The applied definition of a learning contract was: 'A Learning Contract is an agreement for a programme of future study negotiated between the student, the employer and the polytechnic.' Students have the option of studying any appropriate module through a learning contract approach.

A contract need not match an existing module exactly, although, if it is being used as a prerequisite for future modules this must be taken into consideration. There is no set credit value for a contract, nor a set length of time. The level, credit value, time-scale, content and assessment method will all be agreed when the contract is drawn up between the normal teacher of the module, the student and the employer. {243}

Students are accountable for producing something of value to the employer, and for learning new material over the course of the contract. Employers are accountable for ensuring that the student's learning needs and interests are given time and attention. Experience has demonstrated just how challenging this can prove to students:

> Most students felt that a contract had been a more difficult mode of study than the traditional method and that it required considerable motivation and perseverance. {243}

Preparation for a capability approach is essential.

> Evaluation of the pilot scheme has led to the conclusion that students need to be prepared for this degree of self-directedness, especially if they are to be rigorous in their approach. A key issue in the success of contracts could well be the selection of motivated students with a good track record. Students need to be made aware that this is likely to be a more difficult mode of study. Setting an initial hurdle, such as the production of a brief, might help to ensure more dedicated effort. Groups of students can be self-supporting, which could cut tutorial support. Readily available distant learning material could also assist. The role of the employer in terms of help and advice also needs to be clearly identified in the contract. {243}

Also at Wolverhampton Polytechnic, students on the BSc (Hons) Computer Science {241} and other courses have the option of taking a module on business information processing during the final year. Teaching and learning methods, working arrangements and assessment procedures were determined by ongoing negotiation between staff and students. By the end of this module, students were required to demonstrate a critical understanding and the ability to apply project management techniques to the development of large-scale software products. Each week a regular one-hour meeting was held to discuss the previous class and to plan the next. A written plan and report was produced each week.

Prior to this programme students experienced a year of industrial placement. This motivated them to wish to exercise more control over their learning and to use the skills they had acquired at work. This module provided the opportunity to draw together technical knowledge from previous modules in relation to project management, operating in teams and managing people.

> Negotiation is a key factor in these processes and thus was appropriate as
> the central tenet in this module. {241}

**Staff had gained confidence in student-centred methods of teaching and
learning through Enterprise in Higher Education workshops.**

This example addresses common concerns of engineering academics
to ensure coverage of particular content areas. In the case of this example,
the broad content of the module was not open to negotiation. This
included project planning and control, project estimation and costing,
quality assurance and reliability, system life cycle and maintenance and
systems analysis and design. The basic assessment strategy was also
predetermined.

- *Assignment 1:* an individual critical review of an appropriate topic.
- *Assignment 2:* a group assignment based on the application of knowledge and skills to a problem set out in the form of a case study.

Both elements were required to have written and oral components. What
was open to negotiation included:

- teaching and learning methods;
- order of material;
- assessment content (within the above constraints);
- assessment weighting;
- assessment marking (self/peer/staff);
- selection of teams; and
- mechanisms for negotiating.

**Even with these clear parameters, the challenges to students were con-
siderable.**

> The actual negotiation was the most difficult part of the process during the
> first year. Students tended to opt for safe traditional methods such as
> standard lectures and had to be encouraged to select more enterprising
> modes of work. A number of group activities were devised, the most
> successful being the formal review of the project schedule which each team
> had devised. {241}

After the first year of this programme, the course team decided to change
the emphasis of negotiation between staff and students to negotiation
primarily between students. This strategy is also well suited to large
groups of students. Students are now allocated to groups of 12 to 15, each

of which functions as an information systems consultancy company. Advertisements are issued for the managing directors' posts, and applications are received freely from the entire student group. Each applicant gives a presentation to other applicants on their suitability for the job. The applicants themselves select the managers required.

Each company is then commissioned to undertake two major information systems projects. The focus and completion of these takes place entirely within the 'company' – in other words, through student/student negotiation. One hour per week is set aside for a formal full company meeting where lecturers attend as observers. Informal sub-groups are held as required. Both oral and written reports are produced by each company. Tutors also now plan to liaise with the information systems managers to determine students' grades, based on the appraisal system agreed among company members.

At the University of Exeter {51}, up to 100 students in the School of Engineering have the advantage of an open learning module in the second year of their engineering degree. This is compulsory and counts towards degree classification. It may, by negotiation, be a non-engineering study or project.

Students negotiate personal study or project programmes, including collaborative initiatives with local industry and commerce. The module leader helps to match what the student wants to do with the support available within and outside the university. Targets and strategies for meeting them are negotiated between tutor and student, with the involvement of external agencies where appropriate. This agreement provides the basis for assessment of achievement.

The module allows for the development of self-awareness in relation to skills such as communication, organization, scheduling and appraisal. The flavour of the module is perhaps best illustrated by a quote from the preliminary note to students.

> The idea behind this module is... to provide an opportunity to practise the skills of setting your own targets, meeting your own deadlines, assessing your own performance, and generally getting organized for serious self-directed learning. We shall ask you to submit your preliminary ideas for open learning, including:
>
> * *targets:* what do you want to do, hope to achieve;
> * *processes:* how do you intend to go for your targets; and
> * *outcomes:* how will you present and evaluate what you have done?
>   {51}

Internally, the decision was taken to locate the module in the second year of a four-year course so that first year skills could be further explored and built on. Colleagues in the department are now exploring the scope for extensions of the capability approach in subsequent years.

Academics in the school of engineering were approached in order to identify their willingness to support students who wished to participate in this scheme. Detailed preparation was provided through individual discussion with the two staff responsible for operating the module.

> The difficulty in introducing such an innovation is in persuading staff to recognize that they have more to contribute to the educational process than just their proven expertise in a specialist field. Tutors can be reluctant to allow students to take real responsibility for devising personal study/project programmes when they do not appear to have 'respectable' technical content. {51}

Experience builds confidence, as the quality of learning is seen to be enhanced.

> The local Chamber of Commerce helped to develop contacts in support of the open learning module. The Industrial Advisory Group that monitors the curriculum of the school of engineering is also supporting the scheme. The science advisers of the Local Education Authority assist in making contacts with schools, to allow for 'peer tutoring' opportunities. Professional and external bodies have generally been supportive and instrumental in developing the open learning module. {51}

Contracts in engineering and technology tend to be informal rather than formal. However, at the Polytechnic of North London, students on a BTEC HND in Science (Polymer Technology) {141} engage in negotiation and planning for a work programme with the Science Museum. The programme is intended to deepen students' grasp of fundamental principles in polymer technology. The specific objectives are for students to:

- study the factors affecting the ageing of celluloid articles;
- determine the nature of the degradation processes; and
- suggest a method to arrest this degradation or storage conditions that will prolong the life of the material.

This development was introduced in response to requirements spelled out by BTEC in its *Policies and priorities into the 1990s* document and subsequent guidelines. In particular, the unit was designed to develop a range of personal, interpersonal and problem-solving skills while at the same time simulating the environment typical of the polymer industry. The Science Museum offered an ideal opportunity for fostering intellectual, professional and teamwork capabilities:

> The Science Museum has a dilemma in trying to preserve articles only designed for relatively short lifetimes, particularly those which are naturally based (eg, cellulose polymers) as opposed to some oil-based polymers. It has limited research resources and the students have limited opportunities to tackle such realistic problems. Thus a preliminary investigation into this problem seemed ideal for students commencing their careers in the polymer field. {141}

Students are challenged to engage in recurring cycles of investigation, group problem solving, negotiation, planning and assessment.

> Students initially visit the Science Museum and a factory currently producing mouldings from nitrocellulose (celluloid). In groups, the students then review the problem and research the necessary background information. After discussion of the project, students devise an investigative action plan. This is negotiated with the lecturer, as well as with peers, with a view to work-load distribution and deadlines. Regular meetings (usually weekly) take place with the staff responsible for the assignment. Each small group discusses its goals and progress towards them.
>
> Assessment takes place at each of these meetings with groups negotiating grades for each member, encompassing peer-, self- and lecturer-assessment together. Members within the group are accountable for reporting regularly to each other, both orally and in writing. They also report to the class as a whole and the lecturers, so ensuring everyone maintains an overview and enabling a discussion on priorities to take place. Formal presentations to the class are also made at specific times during the project.
>
> Each student is obliged to prepare an individual report on their area of the literature review (including communications with relevant companies and other non-library sources of information) together with suggestions for the direction the project would now follow. These are collated to produce a final dossier that backs up a final presentation to peers, lecturers and representatives from the Science Museum. {141}

This example illustrates ways in which students can be involved in major ongoing research projects, through which their intellectual grasp of academic content is given meaning through their experience.

Theme Three: Active and interactive learning

Introduction
Active and interactive learning have become key features of engineering
and technology degrees. Case studies, projects and problem-centred
approaches to teaching provide students with opportunities to integrate
and relate their understanding of pertinent theory and principles, while
developing skills relevant to planning and managing their own learning,
individually and within groups. Increasingly, such activity now involves
collaboration with industry and/or other disciplines.

At Imperial College, London {74}, an alternative approach has been
introduced into the third year vibration analysis course. This example
illustrates the efforts of a lecturer trying to introduce a capability approach, which requires him and the students to navigate their way against
the mainstream currents of the programme as a whole.

The entire course is organized around a set of problems, the solutions
to which are a major part of the assessment. The problems are typical of
those met in industry. Students work in groups and are required to solve
a selection of problems, acting as consultants to a client group. The client
group prepares a critique of the consultants' solution, and discusses it at
an oral presentation session. Roles are reversed for the other problems.
The course is divided into three phases of six to seven weeks, each phase
ending with oral presentations.

This innovation arose out of a single lecturer's concern that an
excessive emphasis was being placed on technical theory at the expense
of students developing an intellectual and practical grasp of real engineering problems. The challenge was to fit the approach into the standard
timetable and to ensure that the work-load was similar to that of conventional courses.

Evaluation confirmed that this was achieved (Cawley, 1989), but
furthermore, as is so often the case when they take more responsibility,
students become more highly motivated and involved.

> Student time input was somewhat greater than their estimates, since stu-
> dents could frequently be heard discussing the problems in the coffee room,
> an almost unknown occurrence on conventional courses.

When introducing an approach that significantly jars with the dominant
culture of teaching and learning, proper preparation of students is vital.
In this case, an introductory session helps students to decide whether or
not to take this option. Formal input consists of four mini-lectures/dem-

onstrations designed to illustrate the way in which systems vibrate, as well as a bibliography and some printed notes.

> The students clearly enjoyed the course and felt that they had learnt as much technical material as they would on a conventional course... The most commonly mentioned features were its focus on real problems, the absence of examination, and the fact that students were treated in 'a mature way'. (Cawley, 1989)

Tutors observed that student enjoyment and skills development were enhanced and:

> ...discussions were more productive and at a higher level than amongst students on conventional courses. Students also were highly motivated and tended to deal with many of the basic issues themselves. The oral presentation sessions also became important learning forums, with incorrect statements being seized on by students, not merely tutors, with clarification through ensuing debate. The retention of points raised in this way also proved to be very high. (Cawley, 1989)

In the Department of Civil Engineering at the University of Bradford {12}, a number of difficulties were identified with the conventional teaching of the second year course in concrete technology and water engineering. Students were not making the necessary connections between these courses and others on the timetable, and were not, for example, appreciating the link between the microstructure of concrete and its in-service performance, or the selection of treatment processes and the desired water quality. It was decided to adopt an industrial pattern of small group problem-based learning.

> Thus, the students are literally confronted with the connections in a more obvious manner, whilst learning both task and process skills. ... the solution to the problem cannot be achieved without making the required connections. The problems increase in complexity, scale, time allocated and academic expectation as the course progresses. Problems set have included a pipeline in the North Sea, a dam site in Scotland and a sewer interceptor scheme loosely based on one built in Edinburgh. {12}

Assessment of student progress is through a combination of written reports, oral presentations, diaries, summaries, essays and short question/answer exercises.

The commitment and initiative of a few staff who bring a clear sense of purpose to the redesign of a programme are often the starting point for more widespread change. In this case, the innovation was also assisted by the provision of Enterprise in Higher Education funding. The lecturers involved in this course development described their stance as follows.

> The *process* (learning how to learn, applying the engineering method) is as important as the *task* (learning the academic content, the scientific principles). It is therefore necessary to equip students with the process skills required for industry-based learning. Traditional engineering teaching has been essentially passive: learning followed by problem. Industrial learning is active with problems being presented without all the necessary knowledge to hand. It is also conducted in small groups working towards an accepted common goal. As such, students need to create and take opportunities, accept responsibility and risks, solve problems, turn ideas into action and work effectively with other people. Desirable as they are, developing these skills does not easily fit the traditional teaching style. {12}

Students are prepared for this problem-based approach through communication skills courses. Aspects of group work such as strategies for problem solving, leadership, oral and technical report presentations, role playing exercises, non-verbal communication and information retrieval are encountered. The support of library and laboratory staff has been identified as critical, lest the learning style being encouraged be 'subverted by a weak link in the chain.' On the whole, the response of students has been positive and encouraging. 'Particularly impressive has been their response to a challenge. The more difficult the issues, the more the students rose to meet them.' {12}

The key lessons learnt from this development are, as described by tutors, that:

- it is essential that the student's creativity is not stifled by the imposition of the teacher's solution at any stage;
- more preparation is required to account for the variety of feasible responses that students can make;
- problems need to be structured to make intermediate goals explicit, so as to sustain motivation; and
- communication skills need to be introduced prior to this programme, rather than in parallel. {12}

At Hatfield Polytechnic {63}, all engineering undergraduate students participate in a one-week interdisciplinary design project during their second year. This is intended to demonstrate how the general principles of design can be applied across several disciplines. A substantially common first year design course provides the foundation for this activity.

Students are brought together in teams which are deliberately interdisciplinary. They have to come to terms with working in a group and with others who have different backgrounds, interests and specialist expertise.

> The design projects are chosen to be realistic, real-life problems which demand contributions from more than one discipline. They require students to think laterally, to exercise initiative and imagination and to come up with a solution within very tight time-scales. Examples have included a vehicle weighbridge, traffic cone laying, litter clearance from canals and a supermarket checkout. {63}

Teams are allocated to staff supervisors whose duties are to encourage, advise and assess. Following two preliminary meetings, all teams have the complete week to plan and carry out the design to satisfy the project brief. The design is a 'paperwork' exercise only, involving sketching, technical drawing, CAD, modelling and calculations. Students are required to present the results of their work to a panel of judges.

> This is required to include a report and a display stand. Issues of cost and implementation are required to be addressed, together with issues such as marketing, ergonomics and public acceptability where relevant. {63}

Also at Hatfield, first year electrical and electronic engineering students {61} undertake project work jointly with diploma students from the Hertfordshire College of Art and Design who are studying three-dimension design and model making. The projects are sufficiently open ended to allow creation of imaginative solutions. They involve the design and construction of a working prototype for a range of potential market areas.

The interdisciplinary project week represents only a small proportion of the overall student work-load in the second year. The influence of this has, however, been seen as pervasive for both students and staff.

> Students found the projects highly motivating both as an exercise in their own right and as a different form of teaching/learning experience. Many students became deeply committed to the success of their projects and put in many hours of additional work. {63}

Substantial benefits have also resulted for staff.

Many have come together in an interdisciplinary context for the first time. It was evident that staff from the different disciplines found the experience of supervising interdisciplinary groups stimulating and valuable. ... an off-campus briefing workshop was offered for those involved in the supervision and assessment of the projects. This generated wider ownership of the idea, and a commitment to making it a success. An annual feedback workshop has enabled staff to reflect on their learning, based on this experience, and to plan improvements for the following year. {63}

At Dundee University, students following the BEng (Hons) Civil Engineering {34} undertake a project to design and build a real bridge for a client. Students define the brief, identify the optimum design and prepare all technical, financial and planning details necessary to build the 10-metre bridge. The bridge is constructed during a week-long residential field trip and must withstand the crossing of agricultural vehicles over a stream on farmland in the highlands.

The design element of the exercise was a compulsory project-based component. The construction element was optional but the majority of students participated. The exercise was split into three separate phases.

(1) problem definition and concept design;
(2) detail design – primary; and
(3) detail design – refinement.

Students work in groups of three for each phase and are required to make an illustrated presentation designed to 'sell' their solution. This is subject to general discussion and appraisal, including consideration of the technical and management decisions controlling the next phase. Students are required to criticize and assess their own work and that of their colleagues. Each group is also required to submit written reports.

This innovation originated with a concern over the extent to which conventional teaching concentrated on analysis with a strong emphasis on numerical calculations in accordance with previously defined procedures:

There is comparatively little emphasis on the wider aspects of problem solving, especially aspects which require critical judgement and decision making by the students – eg, definition of the problem and appraisal of alternatives. If the construction stage is omitted, then there is no opportunity to develop and practise the teamwork skills necessary to achieve completion of any significant project. There is also no opportunity to review the complete project and learn from the implementation phase. {34}

Real problems based on real needs of real clients make it difficult for students to avoid taking the work seriously.

> The exercise provided valuable opportunities for students to draw on knowledge and skills learnt in other aspects of their course – eg, materials, structural analysis, detailing, drawing, report writing, presentations, etc – and apply them in a practical context, thus demonstrating the relevance of their studies and reinforcing the learning process. Besides providing obvious opportunities to develop skills in design and management, it provided practical opportunities to demonstrate and practise concepts which can be difficult to grasp in a classroom situation, such as teamwork, planning for contingencies, safety, accuracy and tolerances. {34}

By the end of the construction phase, a marked increase in general capability and confidence of students was noticeable. Students found the work:

> ...stimulating, hard work and enjoyable. On completion of their degree, many stated that this exercise was the high point of their entire university course. Students found the exercise a very good talking point in employment interviews and employers commented favourably on the exercise and on the way students talked about it. {34}

This development required consideration of staff and student time, the availability of suitable clients and projects, safety/liability issues and finance. (Funding came not only from the university but also from the client and industrial donations arranged with the client's assistance.) Staff also identified a need for wider change.

> Acceptance by university staff appraisal/promotion committees and higher education funding councils of the value of teaching, and positive recognition of quality in teaching (ie, considering excellence in teaching as a valid promotion criterion), is essential to maintain staff enthusiasm and motivation. {34}

Theme Four: Assessment

Introduction
In engineering, conventional examinations have, in the main, traditionally been used to assess the extent to which the students have acquired a command of key principles. There is now, however, a growing development of more varied strategies such as case studies, open-book assess-

ment, project work and self- and peer-assessment. There is also growing attention on the assessment of how students tackle problems, and of their ability to engage in processes that are key to their effectiveness as engineering professionals. For example, teamwork, communication and the ability to take responsibility for their abilities in design and problem-solving activities. Issues of particular interest and debate include the assessment of individuals in group projects, the moves towards criterion-based assessment and general concern over assessment loading on students and staff.

Overall, given the new challenges facing higher education generally, and engineering education in particular, there is much evidence of experimentation with approaches that relate more directly to claimed learning outcomes of engineering programmes and enhance the quality of student learning and involvement.

At Imperial College, London, first year chemical engineering students are involved in a course on problem solving (Higgins et al, 1989). The aim of the programme is to provide an introduction to processes and procedures of problem solving that students can build on in subsequent design and related projects over the duration of their undergraduate course, and subsequently throughout their professional careers.

The course is divided into four stages. In the first stage, they learn about theoretical models for analysing and describing problems. In the second stage, groups of students tackle problems set in a real engineering context. They are obliged to record their progress, on the task and in their work together as a group.

> The first two stages are run in parallel: if the first is done before the second, the students do not see its point; the problem used in the second stage is chosen so that it cannot be solved without the material learned in the first.
> (Higgins et al, 1989)

The third stage confronts students with an artificial problem. The groups observe the process of problem solving adopted by one member of the group. Finally, groups compete to produce a diverse quantity of solutions.

Assessment is based on a detailed project evaluation guide that students submit during the second week.

> Roughly, a third of the marks are given for the technical solution itself, a third for the presentation of that solution and the remaining third for the process by which the problem was solved. ... prompting by staff is necessary

during time-out sessions before a group of students grasps the importance of the marks given for process aspects. Indeed, despite the best efforts of the staff, a few groups never do grasp this. (Higgins et al, 1989)

Lest students confuse the tutors' roles as educators with that of assessors, no work is assessed in the first week.

This has the additional benefit that the students can experiment and make mistakes without penalty. The work in the second week, in contrast, is assessed and counts towards each student's degree grade. (Higgins et al, 1989)

Solutions are presented in a plenary session on the last day of the second week. Wall posters and table displays are reviewed by all before staff undertake the marking, using a project evaluation guide check-list. Each working group then attends a feedback session of about 20 minutes.

The students are taken through their solution and the marking is explained. The same mark is awarded to each member of a group. Staff are aware that at times the allocation of a group mark may be unfair to individuals. Nevertheless, it has always been felt that any attempt to assess individual contributions would be detrimental to the group working as a team. The feedback session is also used to encourage students to reflect on the skills they have developed during the course and how they might use them in future...

Technically, the work which the first year students do is as advanced as work which used to be undertaken by third year students. The presentations which the students make are much more interesting, both for the students to prepare and for the staff to assess, than are conventional reports. The students are much noisier and more sociable in their groups than they ever were when working alone. (Higgins et al, 1989)

Students are perceived by staff who take them in later years to be:

...more capable of devising a wide variety of possible solutions to a problem than previous generations of students who had not taken the course and would have been content with just one. (Higgins et al, 1989)

Lower et al (1982) make the point that the dilemma of how to assess individual contributions to a group effort is not dissimilar to the one faced by industry, where 'a member of a project team has expectations of recognition of individual effort by increase in salary or promotion, or merely praise'. The point is made that this can be pointed out to students to good effect although, in the authors' experience, the traditional emphasis of higher education on grades and competition is difficult to override. But the point is also made that the observation and subsequent assessment of product and process is of central importance when group projects are used.

At Sheffield City Polytechnic {175}, in an integrated engineering programme supported by the DTI, students build up a personal and professional development portfolio. Some sections are for personal reference only; others are designed to provide a focal point for reflection, critical reviews, action planning and general discussions with tutors, careers specialists, and others, including course colleagues and friends. However, the major function of the portfolio is to gather evidence of progress and achievement against a 'professional engineering profile', which includes technical, professional and personal aspects.

Assessment in the final year of a presentation by the student of selected material from this portfolio will contribute 25 per cent of the final degree mark. (The scheme started in October 1990 and the first students will graduate in 1994.) The portfolio not only provides a vehicle for integrating technical, professional and personal development, but also for carrying forward and recognizing achievement in earlier years of the course. Students may also include evidence of achievement from training placements and industry-based project work.

In recent years, there has been growing demand to broaden the range of abilities, knowledge and understanding that are formally assessed. In addition, there has been a shift away from assessments that compare student with student (norm referenced) to those that are based on pre-determined criteria (ie, criterion referenced). Such assessments can be made in relation to negotiated criteria (based on the active involvement of students), and/or on fixed criteria, such as those established by professional bodies, the NCVQ, or academic staff.

On engineering courses, it is now more common for there to be self- and peer-assessment, individual and group projects, presentations and panel assessments (often including employers), work-based profiling (for sandwich years and shorter placements) and open-book examinations.

At Paisley College, on the honours course in technology and management offered by the Department of Mechanical and Manufacturing Engineering {158}, students are prepared for different approaches to assessment through a series of workshops:

These allow the students to develop skills of self-assessment and the students and staff will then discuss and agree the criteria to be used in the assessment of one of their design case studies. The students will be asked to respond to this case study by submitting a report on how they have judged their achievement based on their own agreed criteria. {158}

This recently developed course embeds progressively higher levels of learner responsibility and accountability over the three years.

In year three it is proposed to assign each student a case study with no agreed programme of study. The staff members will assist the student in their work but will not act as experts or arbiters of the student's programme. It is expected that this will be the most difficult of tasks for the staff, to suppress the natural instinct to teach and be prescriptive. {158}

On the Polytechnic South West HND in Civil Engineering Studies course {195}, intake students act as junior members of a consultancy reporting to a 'partner' on the feasibility of constructing a motorway. A total of three reports are required for submission by each team – two essentially summarizing group work and one drafted by individual students. Each submission includes a project diary as an appendix.

Students are informed at an early stage that they will be permitted to take a full set of reports together with notes they have generated during the unit – but no other literature – into the 'open-book' end of unit assessment. The intention is both to focus the students' efforts on acquiring a comprehensive set of 'well-shaped' notes and to ensure fairness of opportunity. An attempt to initiate peer-assessment of submitted reports has also met with a positive student response. {195}

The Polytechnic of East London HITECC course {43} aims to assess excellence of knowledge acquisition and skills of analysis in all four course components through the application of theory to practical situations and life examples. A clear stance on the purposes of assessment is taken.

Breadth and depth of knowledge are not so important as the demonstration of understanding of the subject, its applications and relevance to work and life. Capability skills are seen as integral to this. {43}

Various aspects of a student's capability are assessed through multiple sources, including:

- establishment of attainable goals through the study contract;
- planning and organizing skills through the management of study and assessment submission;
- exploring and accounting for relevance of studies through critical analysis of the role of new technology component studies, a specialist project and a work placement assessment;
- self-monitoring of progress against agreed criteria based on negotiation of a timetable for goals and submission of feedback from continuous assessment;

- evidence of achievement through the completed portfolio of the year's work, the final critical review of the portfolio and laboratory notebooks; and
- acceptance of responsibility through meeting targets, observing an agreed study timetable and receiving no penalty points for late submission.

Conclusion

Recent developments in engineering education have much to offer colleagues within the field, as well as those in other disciplines. This is well illustrated by the examples submitted to the authors, only a fraction of which it has been possible to include.

Engineers face a complex and sometimes conflicting set of demands in terms of access, recruitment, employers' needs, motivation, expansion of the subject base and the rapid pace of technological change. The shift from an elite to a mass system of higher education has posed particular challenges in engineering because of its resource intensive laboratory-based disciplines.

Implicit in the examples is a recognition of changing priorities, in terms of the skills and qualities that a capable engineer in future will require and how these might best be developed.

The many examples of capability approaches now emerging in engineering education deserve widespread attention. In this chapter we have tried to pay tribute to some of the work that is not as widely published as it should be. The debate that we hope will ensue can, in turn, stimulate further developments that can continue to enhance the quality of engineering education in Britain.

References

Ball, Sir Christopher (1989) *More Means Different*. London: RSA.
Ball, Sir Christopher (1991) *Learning Pays*. London: RSA.

Bonwitt, B. (1990) 'Steps Courses in the Universities.' In: *Engineering Futures*. The Engineering Council, RSA and The Training Agency.

Cawley, P. (1989) 'The Introduction of a Problem-based Option into a Conventional Engineering Degree Course.' *Studies in Higher Education,* 14, 1, pp. 83–95

The Engineering Council (1985) *Raising the Standard.*

The Engineering Council (1990) *Continuing Education and Training Report.*

The Engineering Council and Standing Conference on University Entrance (1988) *Admissions to Universities: Action to Increase the Supply of Engineers.*

Entwistle, Noel, Hounsell, D. et al (1989) *The Performance of Electrical Engineering Students in Scottish Higher Education.* Department of Education, University of Edinburgh.

Higgins, J. S., Maitland, G. C., Perkins, J. D. and Richardson, S. M. (1989) 'Identifying and Solving Problems in Engineering Design.' *Studies in Higher Education*, 14, 2, p. 169.

HMSO (1980) *The Finniston Report.* HMSO, Cmnd 7794.

HMSO (1987) *Higher Education: Meeting the Challenge.* HMSO, Cmnd 114.

HMSO (1991) *Higher Education: A New Framework.* London: HMSO, Com 1541.

Lower, B., Coulthurst, A., Blount, G. N. and Elcock, D. (1982) 'Assessment of Group Projects.' *European Journal of Engineering Education*, 7, pp. 171–87.

Macaulay, C. (1990) 'The Experience and Performance of Electrical Engineering Students in Scottish Higher Education.' In: *Engineering Futures*. The Engineering Council, RSA and The Training Agency.

Parry, G. (1990) 'Introduction and Conference Report.' In: *Engineering Futures*. The Engineering Council, RSA and The Training Agency.

PCAS (1991) News release No. 2 on 1991 entry.

Smithers, A. (1990) 'Patterns of Participation in Engineering Higher Education.' In: *Engineering Futures*. The Engineering Council, RSA and The Training Agency.

Sparkes, J. J. (1989) *Quality in Engineering Education.* Engineering Professors' Conference Occasional Paper No. 1.

Sparkes, J. J. (1991) *The Future Pattern of 1st Degree Courses in Engineering.* Engineering Professors' Conference Occasional Paper No. 3.

Chapter Six
Capability Through Humanities and Social Sciences

Susan Weil and David Melling

Introduction

Different models of higher education

Many different models of higher education have emerged during its long history. The process has been seen, for example, as one of personal development in face-to-face dialogue with an expert mentor, guide and critic; as a system of training for entry into a learned profession culminating in a rite of admission; as the assimilation by the student of the basic content and essential methods of a specialist discipline as they are expounded by expert lecturers; and as an individual quest for knowledge, understanding and insight in relation to which institutional provision is an array of resources and the final award a by-product.

Sometimes, one model is used to ground the critique of another, sometimes different models are realized side by side in the practice of the same institution, sometimes practice draws on elements typical of different models which may or may not combine coherently.

In the last hundred years there has been a substantial change in the nature and population of higher education institutions in Great Britain. Higher education is no longer the province of a narrow clericy preparing for specialist professional functions, nor is it the finishing school of the upper classes. Models tacitly based on such functional assumptions have become anachronistic, as have models based mainly on the direct continuation of schooling. Students now arrive in HE institutions at a wide variety of ages, from a wide variety of backgrounds and with a wide range of prior experience: they arrive with very different ambitions and aspirations, and increasingly institutions see it as their role to enable the realization of these.

Developments in humanities and social sciences education

In the humanities and social science disciplines, the widening age range and background of the intake has had a particularly tangible impact. Patterns of provision have been questioned and renegotiated; student aspirations and student opinion have become a significant element of the planning and evaluation agenda. Established assumptions as to the central importance of curricular coherence, integrity and progression have been questioned, and the significance of the student's own activity as a learner has attained greater recognition.

Specific aspects of the history of the humanities and social sciences can sometimes give the impression of cumulative and incremental progress, but this does not reflect the fundamental logic of these disciplines. They are not stable, unitary, clearly differentiated bodies of object matter, method and theory. Their methodologies are open to critique and are in principle controvertible, the nature and limits of their content are arguable and not predetermined, their boundary definitions and interdisciplinary barriers are constructed, are perceived to be so, and are therefore negotiable. The nature of these disciplines is neither precise nor coherent nor stable. They lend themselves to radical reconstruction of theory and practice, and allow for fundamentally different and frequently irreconcilable approaches to co-exist within the same field of activity.

These features can be seen as inherent strengths that have continued to be valued in humanities and social science education, including by employers (CIHE, 1990; CNAA, 1990). They also offer a framework into which capability principles and practices can be integrated.

Learning processes and intended outcomes: traditional and evolving

Students seeking a higher education in humanities and social science disciplines are normally required as an essential part of their course to acquire and develop a range of interpretative, analytic and critical skills. It is not sufficient for students to be able to ingest, recall, understand, assimilate and represent accurately bodies of evidence, argument and theory handed out by teachers, though even these activities can contribute something to the development of capability. The student is expected to go beyond such a limited and passive role and to participate in academic activities typical of the disciplines he/she studies.

Academics in the humanities and social sciences have become accustomed to seeing themselves and their disciplines as the object matter of their own and each other's critical and analytic study and theoretical interpretation. They are used to challenging the fundamental values and methods of their disciplines, and such questioning is given prominence even at an undergraduate level. In this way, the disciplines students study are themselves problematized within the curriculum.

Contemporary students of the humanities and social sciences enter into a complex conversation to which they are invited to make their own personal contribution, albeit traditionally in the local and relatively private forum of the seminar, the simulation exercise, the report, the essay and the examination paper. The student is invited by the very nature of the disciplines, by their present state and by the ways they interrelate, to become an active participant, not a passive observer.

Typically, courses in the humanities and social sciences have tended to move away from a normative definition of core content, and have given progressively greater recognition to the role of student choice and the value of student autonomy in the individual's determination of his/her specific programme of studies. There has been a lesser but significant degree of recognition of student activity in shaping approaches to both methods and criteria of assessment. Interesting developments of this kind are represented among the examples discussed in the following sections.

Opening the variety of ways students can present their work and their outcomes, and especially opening the method and medium of presentation (and perhaps the criteria for its assessment) to negotiation directly enhances the level and significance of the student's active participation and promotes the development of skills not necessarily at issue elsewhere in the curriculum.

Students' interests and experiences as the starting point for learning
The increasing realization that the curriculum need not necessarily be determined by, and certainly need not be limited to, a fixed canon of content, progressively opens up the opportunity for increasing exploitation of students' learning and experience prior to entry on a particular course. Recognition of the value of prior learning can vary from making the student's prior experience the object-matter of study within the course, to allowing the negotiation of course elements which build directly on the student's specific prior experience, to the allocation of a formal credit value to the student's prior learning as contributing to the award sought.

Opening the curriculum to the recognition of the value of prior learning helps develop a more positive policy for access that is not limited to allowing new groups into a static system, but allows the system itself to develop in order to meet the needs – and fully exploit the talents, skills, capacities and resources – of all students.

Combining study and employment

Just as curriculum designers can take on the challenge of recognizing the value of students' prior experience and of allowing it to contribute directly to the structure and content of the student's course, it is equally possible for a student to combine study and employment in such a way that the student is employed to do something which is itself part of the course. This has long been familiar in one sense in terms of the use of periods of paid placement. New initiatives go significantly further, to allow, for example, the possibility of a part-time student carrying out tasks in a professional capacity which are at the same time projects assessed and credited within the course structure, or to allow a full-time student to take on a formal consultancy role for a client, the negotiation, design and presentation skills being then assessed side by side with the academic value of the product.

Instrumentalism vs liberalism: a meaningful dichotomy?

Student numbers in the humanities and social sciences have never been so high. At the same time, the pressures to absorb wholesale the currently fashionable emphasis on relevance and intrumentalism are growing. While it would be supine for educators to accept uncritically a demand that they provide courses which produce graduates tailored to fit the immediate needs of the employment market, students stand only to gain from the extra emphasis on learner responsibility and accountability as the basis for the development of personal, social and communicative skills and a range of transferable skills which enhance their employability, their capacity for self-employment, their entrepreneurship and their ability to contribute to the development of society, be it as parent, worker or citizen. Ronald Barnett puts the case eloquently:

> Insisting on the imaginative, creative and critical components of a genuinely open learning experience will go much of the way to enabling students to fulfil their potential throughout the rest of their lives. This means, equally, that the appropriate design of the curriculum cannot be simply read off the world as it is now and in particular off the economy and its associated institutions. (Barnett, 1989)

Indeed, one might well question the soundness of a system which defines its notion of education so narrowly that it sees no need for remedial intervention when faced by students who show high academic competence, write intelligent, critical, original work, but remain completely at a loss when faced with the need to communicate ideas verbally, to share in group activities, to define their own educational objectives, to present and argue a case or to show evidence of the array of skills needed if they are to make their way in the world at large.

An enhanced respect for student autonomy should not entail an abdication from the need to intervene critically to promote a student's self-development as an effective communicator, a successful teamworker and a responsible planner. The conversation that grounds the relationships that are central to study in this field must begin with a respect for students' needs and aspirations. It must also provide the means whereby all parties to the dialogue, students and tutors alike, can be challenged and changed.

The fundamental objectives of the Capability initiative are to promote student autonomy and responsibility in the learning process, to enhance active learning, co-operative interaction and effective communication. Taking on board the challenges of the Capability project should not, however, lead to a simplistic identification of instrumental value with process and intrinsic value with content, still less to the acceptance of process as transferable and content as not. Knowledge can be transferable as well as skills.

Study in the humanities and social sciences does not simply enable the development of skills and knowledge. Students' perceptions, feelings, emotions, sensibilities, attitudes, value assumptions and value commitments are also liable to development and change, though this rarely appears as a key issue in non-professional areas of study. The twinned emphasis on responsibility and accountability enables such outcomes, and the processes whereby they might be developed, to be made more explicit.

Theme One: Reviewing and building on experience

Students are increasingly mobile. As structures change to promote wider access, potential and existing students will have greater freedom to make use of higher education learning opportunities in different ways, and for different purposes. Opening up higher education to more and different students in itself makes any notion of a homogenous student population a thing of the past. Mature students study in humanities and social sciences more than any other field. The positive value humanities and social sciences teachers place on breadth of background and prior experience adds to the attractiveness of these areas to mature students.

Humanities and social science disciplines have long accepted students who have neither 'relevant' experience nor A level preparation in either a specific or related subject. Well before the days of CATS and APEL, many humanities and social sciences departments made arrangements to accept students through 'non-traditional' routes. Such developments are now made a positive virtue in the competition for students. As a more diverse range of students engages in humanities and social sciences study, the challenge of their varying aspirations, backgrounds, and learning interests becomes sharper.

Courses already exist which illustrate ways in which students' interests and experience, their experiential 'bodies of knowledge' and informally constructed theories, can be respected from the point of entry.

It is often said that traditional A level entry students are the most difficult to persuade to take more responsibility for their own learning. When students on the BA (Hons) in European Studies/Italian at the University of Kent {76} expressed dissatisfaction with the range of material concerning Italian culture and civilization that they had been able to cover during their A level courses, their dissatisfaction provided the basis for introducing a capability approach. Class meetings were devoted to discussing which aspects of Italian culture and civilization would interest students and why. Groups were made responsible and accountable for searching out sources and relevant information, and presenting the outcomes of their enquiry to class members. This work represented about one quarter of the course programme. Monitoring was done by report and essay writing, seminar work and oral discussion. Some limited experiment in self-evaluation was also attempted.

> Students took the challenge seriously. Some went out looking for sources and bibliography. Others concentrated on producing a brief outline of what they would have liked to study individually. Tasks were then prepared for the whole term, with basic bibliographical references and an emphasis on teamwork. For example, two or three students were to work on each particular aspect of the programme. {76}

The Certificate in Community Studies at Leeds Polytechnic {90} is a part-time modular course for adults with experience of paid or unpaid work in the community. The course is based on a minimum of formal lecturing and a maximum of student activity through pair and group work. Personal study materials and focused assignments support student-directed learning. Students can also make up their programme from a range of interdisciplinary modules within the social sciences and hu-

manities leading to a Diploma or BA (Hons) in Social and Community
Studies. Assessment is based on an assignment structured around a
learning contract that focuses on a 'live' issue and is to be carried out
wherever possible in conjunction with relevant organizations outside the
polytechnic. The topics, objectives and criteria for evaluation of the
contract are negotiated between students and tutor.

At Teesside Polytechnic {216} students on a BTEC HND/C in Public
Administration work in syndicated groups to create the content of their
syllabus. They do this through researching, discussing and writing and
making presentations on how Social Services meet the needs of specified
client groups. Syndicate group members are allocated and, over the year,
rotate through the following roles:

- team leader and report editor;
- oral presenter;
- researcher; and
- critical researcher (foreseeing criticisms and questions likely to arise
  in discussion).

Between 36 and 60 students work in nine teams to cover five social
services and four client groups. Students in each syndicate group make
a learning contract with each other, and produce a 'team diary' as an
appendix to their report. They are actively encouraged to make use of
their peers and of extra-institutional resources. Time is built into the
timetable and rooms made available for groups to meet with or without
a tutor (their choice). Every item of work produced is included for
assessment purposes. By the end of the module, each team is in possession of a library of contemporary social policies that the course as a
whole has created.

The sophisticated organization of student interaction ensures each
group interacts with every other, that student reports are duplicated and
circulated, that each group report is appraised, assessed, augmented, so
that 'an exchange of student created information takes place'.

A group-work diary system was also introduced, to help students,
make learning contracts with each other and plan group activity. As a
further aid to this group, each group had a staffed tutorial about a month
prior to the presentation for guidance both on source of information and
how to approach the task.

Critical to this approach are firstly the guidance given to the student
with regard to the standards expected and, secondly, the system of
feedback which disseminates information about both content and levels

of skill performance – this is an integral part of the student learning process as the feedback forms part of each report exchanged between student groups.

Since 1990, students on a BA (Hons) in Contemporary Studies at Humberside Polytechnic {72} have been prepared from the outset to engage in the research activities of outside agencies. Year one students participate in a workshop course which equips them with necessary skills, including those of communication, self-presentation and self-awareness. They then participate – on a paid basis – in projects negotiated by the college staff, the experience and reports from which are used for integrated assignments on the workshop course.

During the second year, students themselves negotiate links with outside agencies, and engage in research projects as part of their work placement during the summer term. Ten students, for example, were employed to carry out a tenant satisfaction survey for a local housing association. Eight of them organized and completed a sample survey of face-to face interviews and the other two carried out an in-depth case study of two hostels, one for young, single people and the other for those with learning difficulties. The first year students involved were all studying a Housing Studies course on the Contemporary Studies degree. This research therefore gave them an insight into how a housing association operates and the type of tenants involved. They were able to use their skills to help the association monitor and evaluate the service it provides. The report was assessed for information technology skills and for a critical evaluation of the methodology employed. The assignment also provided the opportunity for the student to reflect on his or her contribution to the project.

This particular approach, which allows for the involvement of students in the research process for outside agencies, can work well on a consultancy basis, but this course team has encountered difficulties in applying these ideas in shorter work placement experience for a larger number of students. It is often reported that considerable time and effort is required to convince employers that they, as well as the student, will benefit from such experience.

In the Department of Nursing, Health and Community Studies at Bournemouth Polytechnic, students on the foundation programme of a BSc (Hons) in Clinical Nursing {10} use problem-based learning to reflect on their clinical practice experience. In this way, its validity as an integral part of their overall learning is emphasized. In groups, they research problems which have come to their attention in the ward setting.

Group members decide their own objectives for the day, and agree whether and how to make use of staff resources. The students have a log book that provides starting points for learning – such as topics for group inquiry – but its main purpose is for the students to complete a record of their own observations and investigations.

The introduction of this innovation at first seemed to prompt student resistance. This is a common theme in lecturers' accounts of beginning to pass over more responsibility to students. This reaction can undermine the confidence of lecturers who can already feel that they are swimming against the mainstream. Student resistance was not, however, what it initially seemed.

> An evaluative exercise with the students at the end of the first term after this innovation began (September, 1990) showed that they were not comfortable with the way it was working. However, the problems identified were connected with the way the students were grouped and the subjects they investigated rather than a problem of working independently of the lecturer. This will be tackled by looking more carefully at how students are introduced to this way of working. {10}

This example underlines the importance of due care and attention being paid to preparing students for a different approach to learning. The uncertainties and lack of confidence that can affect even experienced adults when charged with taking responsibility for their own learning cannot be underestimated.

Allowing students' own interests and their prior experience to be a major element in curriculum construction creates a new kind of partnership between students and lecturers. If the context of that partnership is a co-operative, team-based approach to knowledge acquisition and critical analysis which draws on a variety of methods of negotiating the curriculum, it becomes possible for fundamental questions of student responsibility and accountability to be addressed in new ways, and for a shared evaluation of the character of students' educational experience and of the responsiveness and rigour which are concrete elements in the quality of that experience. These elements are constituted by the specific roles students play, the nature of the tasks they undertake, the character of the negotiations in which their aims become actualized and tasks determined, the nature of the products they present for criticism and assessment and the ways in which that assessment takes place.

Theme Two: Planning, negotiation and approval

While it is rare to find whole courses or whole years of courses based entirely on learning contracts, contract elements of various degrees of formality are common, though not always identified as such. A direct focus on the negotiation of learning contracts highlights the role of students as active autonomous learners, defining their learning goals in a context that demands responsibility and accountability.

A modular structure may give students more responsibility for choosing their own path through a programme of set offerings. In itself, however, it does not guarantee that students will have opportunities for being responsible and accountable for their learning within and across modules. The example that follows illustrates how a modular approach can be used to address that very issue.

At Wolverhampton Polytechnic {248}, optional modules are offered under the Enterprise in Humanities programme to students on the BA/BSc (Hons) Modular Degree and Diploma Scheme. Students are offered a framework within which to identify the skills and abilities they wish or need to develop in relation to future employment while studying the humanities. Examples include:

- being organized;
- using time effectively;
- communicating effectively in different situations;
- planning and thinking ahead;
- working with others to achieve a goal;
- acting with self-confidence; and
- handling conflict and differences of opinion.

Having assessed their learning needs, students are accountable for devising and implementing a structured programme, based on group projects, to deliver agreed learning outcomes. Five modules are offered at levels one, two and three. Various approaches are used to equip students for self- and peer-directed learning. The negotiation and validation of learning agreements take different forms during this three-year optional strand of the enterprise modules, enabling students to become progressively more responsible and accountable over the course of their degree.

Modularity enables students to determine their own meaning for academic coherence; capability modules can make that coherence personally meaningful. Opportunities for student responsibility and accountability provide the 'grouting' that enables students to relate their learning to their own development, and the world within which they live and work.

In the case of Wolverhampton, students are not thrown in at the deep end but, rather, are progressively prepared to set goals and to identify criteria against which they can review progress and performance.

In year one, initial preparation for this way of working is supported by a student/staff manual. This introduces each topic, suggests further reading and gives a selection of structured exercises. The manual includes a list and description of 38 key competences to guide students in their skills development. In future, it is intended to provide this module through a resource-based learning approach derived from the manual. {248}

Students are also helped to become familiar and confident with the negotiation and assessment of learning agreements through a variety of exercises and tasks. All tasks and subsequent group projects are assessed 50 per cent for process, 50 per cent for product/outcome.

Extensive consultation with local school and college teachers, access course tutors, HMI and employers was undertaken during the development of this programme. But although positive support was received from HMI and, in the early stages, employers:

...it has been difficult to maintain employer involvement to the extent the team anticipated and this confirms the general picture reported by higher education in relation to employer involvement in teaching and learning. {248}

As more institutions draw heavily on employer and community resources, interest in familiar programmes can flag in favour of new ones. Employers need to recognize the impact that their withdrawal of interest can have on such developments, including staff and student morale. Moreover, their withdrawal reduces the options for negotiation that the student may identify as important to their own development and career aspirations.

The principles and practices of enterprise learning are currently diffusing to other subject areas within the School of Humanities and Social Sciences, as staff and students recognize the increased emphasis given to personal and interpersonal competences and skills in the workplace. Students of geography, history and media/communications, for example, now recognize the prominence given to such competences and skills in recent and planned curriculum development initiatives.

At Crewe and Alsager College of Higher Education {32} in the Division of Applied Social Studies, 120 full-time and 15 part-time students (on average) undertake 60 per cent of their final year through independent study. They are prepared for this during the first and second years of their degree, when such study represents 27 per cent of these years' work. This tends to take the form of methods, skills and project work that can support students' different pathways through the degree. During the final year, with only general supervision, students undertake a fully negotiated programme. They plan and implement their studies, including the nomination of the method of assessment. In addition, students may choose from a range of modular units to support their independent study programme.

Mature students, especially those who were failed by the education system the first time around, can be positively attracted by programmes that give priority to their needs and concerns. This course was developed as part of the college's response to changing social and education needs, including employment. In particular, it was designed to be of special benefit to women, students from social groups who have not previously benefited from higher education, and other categories of mature students without formal entry qualifications. A major attraction of the programme is its scope for integrating work experience within the context of studying social sciences. This provides the opportunity for students to relate theory to practice. A more recent innovative development is the registration of part-time students' own work-based projects for the award of the degree.

Since September 1989, independent study has been offered as a third year option for Manchester Polytechnic {118} students taking history as part of the BA (Hons) Humanities/Social Studies degree and the BA (Hons) Historical Studies degree. Students spend the equivalent of three hours' class contact time (approximately half a day per week) for 22 weeks in the autumn and spring terms.

Contracts are drawn up between client, student and tutor. These identify the scope of the projects, the manner of assessment, and the ways in which the project seeks to meet the needs of all three parties. Students are accountable for producing interim progress reports, written in a business style, midway through the course, as well as a final report and/or product at the end of the course. Examples of work undertaken thus far include:

- A disk and catalogue history of Cheadle for the Stockport libraries and the organization of a library display of selected materials, now published by the library and available for any interested user.
- Archive material for Stott Benham Ltd, a firm of catering equipment manufacturers, was organized and appropriate publicity material was developed. This was reported in the company's journal.

- Manchester Region History Review: A student undertook a comparative study of the financial management strategies used by local history journals.
- A report on all educational initiatives undertaken by the Manchester Chamber of Commerce since 1885 was prepared, as was an article that summarized the conclusions of the project, and this was published in the Chamber's monthly journal.
- Salford Museum: Materials appropriate to the development of a local heritage industry and held at various locations throughout Salford were catalogued and summarized in a report.
- Manchester Airport: an inquiry into the development of the airport, based on materials held by the Manchester Chamber of Commerce. {118}

The decision to revise the history degree programme was stimulated by the heated general debates about its economic relevance in the late 1980s and early 1990s.

Course planners became challenged to introduce innovations that would improve the quality of provision without undermining the merits of more conventional approaches to history study. More attention began to be paid to *how* what was claimed in the course objectives, such as the development of skills, was actually achieved through the teaching and learning strategies adopted. It was agreed that students ought to have more control over their own education. {118}

Some subjects can easily boast of an emphasis on work placements and practical skills. This was not the case in history. Non-utilitarian and non-vocational values were central to its academic identity. At the same time, the study of history, and of the humanities and social studies generally, was seen to incorporate opportunities to develop a wide range of historical skills. These involved technical skills as well as those of analysis, evaluation and communication. But there were few chances for students to apply these in historical work outside academic institutions.

A wide range of strategies was used to woo appropriate employers to involve themselves with this initiative. These included direct approaches as well as feature articles and advertisements in local newspapers and journals, including those produced by local Chambers of Commerce. Students themselves were also encouraged to take the initiative in identifying and persuading employers. Students and employers were helped to understand clearly the many possibilities for historical work in the community. Long term-projects were also offered, so that the work of one student could be continued in subsequent years: for example, a series of library handbooks and displays.

Emphasizing the role of negotiation in the curriculum highlights issues of student responsibility and accountability, and the crucial dimensions of the modes of autonomy demanded by a capable and reliable person working co-operatively with others. The emphasis on client-orientated activities helps to establish and develop partnerships between the universities and a wide variety of commercial, industrial, cultural and charitable institutions in their region; such connections, apart from their obvious use in extending the reputation of the institution and its courses, and the possible spin-off of opening employment possibilities for students, can have a particular use in renegotiating the ways in which the external clients perceive the value of humanities and social science disciplines and their products. Promotion of capability is also the promotion of quality – quality experienced as enhanced capacity for decision making, autonomous action and responsible execution of tasks.

Theme Three: Active and interactive learning

Traditional approaches to teaching – lectures, seminars and tutorials – have a long and respected history, but they can sit uneasily with notions of active and interactive learning, which emphasize the need for students to grapple with academic material on their own terms, and in ways that develop their capability. Courses have often operated as a collection of individuals working separately. This is at odds with the understanding of societal and cultural processes that is the focus of study in this field. More simply, they are not typical of life or work.

Such tensions have come to be experienced with greater force in recent years within humanities and social sciences higher education. This is not only because of the great influx of mature students coming from a wide diversity of backgrounds, but also as a consequence of issues that are at the forefront of contemporary debates in this field. New developments emphasize students' active construction of meaning, individually and in groups, both in relation to academic material and in relation to their own concerns, interests and aspirations.

Active and interactive learning have a place in long-standing subject traditions as well as in emerging ones. Initial steps can be small. For some, the concern is to find alternatives to lectures and seminars, within traditional course structures, or approaches that complement and extend such offerings. Case studies, simulations and experiential exercises help students engage more actively with academic material, at deeper and more meaningful levels. Others are experimenting with students taking more responsibility for the planning, contents and processes of lectures and seminars.

Reports, articles, presentations, portfolios, videos/tapes/films, radio programmes and exhibitions frequently replace or supplement the more familiar essays, seminar papers and dissertations. Emphasis on active learning suggests a new emphasis on the process of production and on the value of the product. Students' critical appreciation of what they have produced is enhanced when the product has a real audience or client. Submitting an essay to be marked is a different experience from making a presentation to a client or producing a video for practical use.

The learning possibilities of field placements, long a hallmark of study in social or community work, are being mined more effectively, as more explicit attention is being paid to active and interactive learning processes and programme outcomes. Projects too, more likely to be found in vocational subjects in recent years, are also making their own distinctive mark on students' learning experiences in the humanities and social sciences. These can be subject based, but more and more are employer or community based, as students seek to relate their studies to their own questions and purposes.

In the School of English at Birmingham Polytechnic, a BA (Hons) modular degree in English {5}, with 208 full-time and 60 part-time students has first semester modules which emphasize 'doing' rather than 'absorbing'. An emphasis on computer-aided text creation not only builds word-processing skills, but also emphasizes that students are:

> ...active producers of texts rather than merely readers and the traditional reverent distance in English studies between producers and consumers of literature is broken down. {5}

Workshops and the production of portfolios are also a central part of the first year, to establish from the outset the principles of group-managed and independently organized study.

- The 'Case study of a contemporary author' module (year one) disabuses students of the notion that there is a body of knowledge to be 'covered' or a canon of great authors to be taught. Set texts are resources to be drawn on and the authority that is traditionally attributed to them is dislodged through an 'issues-directed' approach to teaching and learning. The only teacher-centred session is a single lecture at the end of the course.

- In 'European poetry in translation', the module tutor acts as editor of an anthology produced by students, whose contributions form their assessment, the course being represented by the investigation which led up to the poetry selection or the critical summary. {5}

To serve the needs of part-time students, the course team has developed distance learning packages, telephone consultation sessions and detailed feedback sheets to accompany course work. Increases in full-time student numbers is seen by this course team as a major influence on the:

> ...demise of the small group tutorial, much beloved by English courses and students but perhaps fostering an unhealthy dependence on the tutor. Full-time students no longer have weekly sessions with personal tutors. Instead, they are encouraged to use staff as resources to draw on to help them organize their studies, facilitate their learning and plan their careers. Year tutors help them draw up self-profiles which assess their skills needs and monitor their progress towards fulfilling them at different stages of the course. Module tutors make themselves available for consultation sessions where they negotiate the exact form the students' assessment will take in that area. {5}

Responding to these pressures with more emphasis on student-centred learning has generated unexpected spin offs. For example, 'writers in residence' have always been a key resource. Their role as facilitators and resource people is being opened up in new ways.

> Writers in residence are facilitators, editing student anthologies, producing their plays as well as advising and encouraging on an individual basis. The resource model, though, has extended far into the classroom teaching on the course itself. Much 'class contact' time is now in the form of 'workshops', classes whose name and function preceded such 'hands-on courses' as 'computer-aided text creation' which would seem more obviously to deserve the title. {5}

At Thames Polytechnic, {218} 'Channel Four' is the name given to a new dimension on the BA (Hons) Humanities programme. Second year students have the opportunity to develop analytical skills in their core studies either with techniques and knowledge drawn from subjects outside the humanities or by extending existing areas of interest into new fields. They select two short courses which include work from across a range of areas including: information technology, social/political survey work, contemporary issues in science and society, and cultural production. Recent offerings include:

> video production; alternative energy resources; drama in performance; writing fiction; before the courts; climatic change; colour, nature and culture; computing in history; forensic science – fact and fiction; miracle workers? (applied chemistry); the concerto; noise pollution; politics of equal opportunities; project management and information technology; science and sociability; and computer-based simulation and modelling. {218}

In the third year, students undertake a collective or individual project, the outcomes of which can be presented in a wide range of forms. The outcome can vary from the traditional long essay to more innovatory forms of work. Creativity is positively valued and the following alternative forms of production are encouraged:

> taped interviews; photographic essays; short fictions; video narratives; drama productions; oral histories; survey reports; bibliographies; essays; collective exhibitions; and desk-top publication. {218}

Working on such projects gives students a more active role in the design of their course. The emphasis on creative production can also enhance students' sense of their responsibility for shaping their education to some of their own intellectual interests and ambitions. A programme such as Channel Four not only offers experience in a range of skills, but also provides students with opportunities to traverse and integrate disciplines. Such emphases, including the integration of science, computing and interactive technologies can heighten confidence in the value of a degree in humanities and its capacity to develop simultaneously a broad yet critical outlook, academic expertise, and student capability.

Theme Four: Assessment

Assessment plays a crucial role in the construction of students' educational experience. It can provide helpful guidance and feedback to students, and help them learn from their experience as they move through a programme. Increasing attention is being paid in the humanities and social sciences to the developmental potential of assessment and to assessment strategies that are congruent with student-centred and capability approaches to teaching and learning, strategies, for example, that in themselves make students more active, and interactive, and stimulate creative and critical thinking and responsible creativity in production.

Assessment of the Independent Study Project in History at Manchester Polytechnic (Theme Three) {118} is negotiated between client, tutor and student.

> A 1000 word interim progress report and the final product carry the weight of marks. The ability of the student to formulate, execute and present the conclusions of a piece of independent work is thus the central skill to be tested, but it is evaluated in the context of the more general skills (analytical, communication, technical, etc). The clients play an integral role in the assessment of their particular students, and are assisted with written and verbal guidance. The students for their part negotiate the weighting and distribution of marks across the various elements that make up their projects and are encouraged to discuss the evaluations of their work at each stage of the assessment. {118}

Monitoring of progress is also achieved through the distribution of questionnaires to clients and students.

Examples of products that have served as the basis for assessment include:

> market surveys and reports; computer software; historical information packs; catalogues of historical records and archives; historical publicity material for companies; historical research for clients; the organization of museum and library displays; articles for company journals or newsletters; historical material on video or cassette; and historical guides. {118}

At Wolverhampton Polytechnic (see Theme Two), on the BA in Cultural Studies Enterprise Modules {246}, an assessment contract is negotiated. Students are responsible for participating in the negotiation of the following:

- statement of competences to be assessed;
- weightings between competences;
- a statement of evidence to be presented to demonstrate competences; and
- allocation of grades between groups and individuals. {246}

Throughout the five modules, students are required to submit one analysis of personal development at the end of each semester and complete skills profiles which incorporate self-, peer- and staff-assessment. The profiles are authenticated and included in the students' final portfolios.

Self-, peer- and tutor-assessment are combined at all stages to provide evaluation of both process and product: how the students work together on the task, and what they produce as a result.

The Enterprise modules are counted towards the award of the BA (Hons) in the same way as other modules, make up one fifth of an undergraduate programme and are detailed on the student transcript.

The introduction of such developments is not without its challenges:

> We are facing other problems which are as yet unresolved: the inadequacies of a summative grading system to reflect the range of learning experiences; problems of assessing and grading group work and individual contributions; and the difficulties students experience in operating peer-assessment. {246}

Final assessment is negotiated and based on presentations of portfolios containing the student's CV, the personal development statement, a critical account of their work shadowing experience, and their interview preparation dossier.

In the School of Languages and European Studies at Wolverhampton Polytechnic {249}, developments in assessment are rooted in the communicative 'revolution' in language teaching and learning that has taken place in schools and in higher education over the past five or six years. A communicative language approach provides students with opportunities to be responsible and accountable for the following:

- extracting information from a range of sources and re-presenting it cogently, for specific audiences and specific purposes, in speech and in writing;
- contributing pertinently to group meetings and helping towards their successful outcome;
- working effectively as a member of a team; and
- doing all the above in a foreign language. {249}

Assessment becomes a key element in the acquisition of communicative skills.

- Assessment is exclusively class-based for oral work.
- Written work is assessed within the routine pattern of course work, not by means of formal examination.
- The assessment criteria must be available to students and gradings discussed with them in terms of these criteria. {249}

Since the communicative syllabus relies to a large extent on effective group work, student performance is frequently judged in terms of the group as a whole, not in isolation. In this specific situation, they are also accountable for the work of the group to which they belong. This is either direct, such as for a task carried out by a given individual by a given date, or more indirect, such as when working with others over a period of time to arrive at a consensus on some issue.

The use of performance criteria places traditional preoccupations with formal language accuracy in a new light. Insofar as structural variety and lexical range increase the communicative impact of the student's performance, they are rewarded. However, these qualities in themselves are of secondary importance within the performance as a whole. In this particular example, arguments used to stimulate changes in approaches to teaching and learning were rooted in changes in the subject itself. The philosophy of communicative competence is used to underpin a shift in the traditional role of tutors, and changes in assessment were summarized as follows:

- The foreign language (FL) is seen primarily as a means of communication and only secondarily, although still importantly, as an object of study. In practical terms, this means that the student uses the FL in order to communicate meanings, to express his/her thoughts and feelings, and to establish and maintain co-operative relations with fellow students.
- Communication must always serve a purpose within the classroom. The listener(s) must need to know what the speaker is attempting to communicate and must be able to negotiate the meaning of the speaker's utterances wherever necessary. This process creates an awareness of both the limits of communication and the need for co-operation in the elaboration of meaning
- Communication is not exclusively a linguistic issue. Grammatical and lexical competence are not in themselves enough, so students must learn the importance of basic interpersonal skills and become conscious of the pragmatic dimension of spoken interaction. 'Communicative competence' is the product of a number of component competences – structural, socio-linguistic and strategic, for example.
- Although what has been said above relates primarily to the spoken language, a communicative syllabus has to devote equal time and attention to promoting successful writing in the FL. Rather than writing simply to display a degree of mastery over the grammar and lexis of the FL, the student learns to write for a particular audience within a particular context. {249}

At the Polytechnic of North London {143}, oral assessment is growing in importance on the Film Studies component of the BA (Hons) Humanities degree. This involves all students, and all units except the Introduction to Film Studies and Project, in small group discussion. Each 'seminar group' will have around 20 students who will be divided into groups of four or five. Assessment relates to work both in the small groups and the large group. Assessment is by tutors:

- by observation of students in groups; and
- using the evidence of students' written summary at the end of the unit on what they have learnt from – and contributed to – the group work.

This has the following aims:

- to emphasize the importance of dialogue as a means of learning the language of the subject, and to indicate to students that staff take this aspect of the work seriously, as an end in itself;
- to nurture the ability to participate in groups that have responsibility for their own learning and organization, and for organizing the activities of the whole group; and
- to develop students' awareness of the processes involved in participating in a group and in learning through discussion. {143}

This mode of assessment currently constitutes 10 per cent of the assessment in all units, except the foundation course. Formalizing this has made it count for students.

The process of change
The above illustrates how once tutors begin to experiment with different approaches to teaching, learning and assessment, they can gradually become open to and excited by new possibilities which, at the beginning, they would not have contemplated:

> The decision to introduce this work came from the film staff group (four members) itself. It followed the decision of the group to abandon examinations in favour of course work. There was a concern to acknowledge the existing practice, to develop it and to indicate its value to students and other staff. Discussions on this led to the possibility of assessing oral work and several discussions led to the drawing up of criteria for assessment (documented both for staff and students). {143}

Similarly, educational values and purposes provided the critical under-pinning to staff involvement in this initiative.

> Assessment of group work was introduced to acknowledge the existing practice of the department, to develop it, to indicate its value to students and other staff, to acknowledge aims of education for capability and to allow for a range of abilities in students. {143}

Change also resulted from new pressures within and outside the institution:

> We were concerned to respond to the general move away from exclusive use of written work as a way of testing students. This development was also in line with equal opportunities policies and approaches developing within the institution. {143}

Opposition was encountered and had to be met with patience and clarity about the educational value of this approach:

> This came from some students and there was peer opposition (largely from other disciplines) or at least scepticism and a concern about resource implications. This was largely overcome by arguing the educational benefits of the activity and assessment in formal committees and consultative meetings. Small group work means students are more active and that they take more responsibility for their own learning. They have an opportunity to practise using the discourse of the subject and to tackle and internalize the discipline's concepts and approaches. This approach also provides the opportunity to learn the cognitive and interpersonal skills involved in group work. {143}

Radical approaches to assessment can, of course, be felt to undermine the quality of awards. However, assessment strategies that draw students into dialogue and negotiation draw on values deeply embedded in humanities and social science disciplines, just as do curriculum structures which draw on students' interests and experience, and promote student activity and interactivity. The shift from student productivity as focused on the execution of standard exercises which are submitted for marking to the creation of products with a real or potential audience, even directed to external clients, re-situates the object presented for assessment and redefines the range of parties with a legitimate voice in the assessment procedure.

Concluding remarks

Students studying humanities and social science disciplines at university level are not expected merely to learn about those disciplines, they are expected to attain a certain competence as practitioners. While there are schools and traditions within disciplines with their own relatively standardized methods and their local dialects, it is nonetheless expected that humanities and social science academics maintain a critical and self-critical attitude to their work and develop a degree of intellectual autonomy in their practice. A capability orientation brings to the fore issues of competence, autonomy and responsibility that reflect the normal self-understanding of practitioners within humanities and social science traditions. The direct address to these issues should enhance the confidence of students and their ability to see themselves as active practitioners involved in their own process of development and supported by more expert practitioners which in turn should underpin the quality of their educational experience.

References

Barnett, R. (1989) *Responsiveness and Fulfilment: The Value of Higher Education in the Modern World*. Abingdon, Oxon: The Higher Education Foundation.

CIHE (1990) *Towards a Partnership: The Humanities for the Working World*. London: Council for Industry and Higher Education.

CNAA (1990) *Humanities and Employment: The CNAA Initiative – Humanities and Employment Briefing 1*. London: Council for National Academic Awards.

Chapter Seven
Capability Through Science and Mathematics

Susan Weil and Ronald Emanuel

The context for change

> Higher education courses in science and technology are... becoming less popular. For many students they provide an unsatisfactory intellectual and educational experience and an inadequate preparation for future jobs. The factual content which has been added over the years has become excessive leading to rote learning and insufficient understanding of fundamental principles.
>
> Many people who would benefit from higher education in science and technology, particularly mature students, cannot do so because of the lack of recognition given to non-traditional qualifications and insufficient practical support. (ACOST, 1991)

This is not a quotation from a group of trend setting educational theorists, but taken from the Report of the Manpower and Training Committee of the Advisory Committee on Science and Technology (ACOST) (1991). ACOST is an advisory committee to the Cabinet. Its Manpower and Training Committee is made up of leaders of science-based industry, university vice-chancellors, and senior Government scientists. If mathematics had been part of its brief, it seems likely that it would have been included in its censure. The ACOST Report recommends that:

> ...higher education institutions implement procedures to audit teaching and place greater emphasis on teaching strategies that enhance understanding, investigative learning, and the development of originality, and the funding councils should take into account the quality of teaching in assessing applications for funds. (ACOST, 1991)

It would be wrong to suggest that there is not much to be proud of in science and mathematics higher education. Despite criticism from some employers, science and mathematics graduates usually end up in fairly well-rewarded employment. But, as ACOST points out, science related subjects in higher education are becoming less popular and are attracting a disproportionately low share of non-standard entrants. ACOST is also correct in identifying the need to enhance understanding, investigative learning, and the development of originality. The Further and Higher Education Act (1992) sets this in the context of responding effectively to more and diverse students while maintaining, if not enhancing, quality.

Going beyond content coverage
Despite the strong case for capability approaches in general, some teachers of science and mathematics in higher education perceive considerable difficulties in introducing a capability approach in their subject area.

There are of course many substantial subject differences within the sciences and mathematics, and care must be taken in generalizing, but much of the apprehension appears to focus on content. The fact explosion continues. Each year scientists and mathematicians see more and more that they could/should/must include in higher education curricula. The pressures to include more and more content appear to be compounded by changes in schools-based teaching of science and mathematics.

Yet the domination of the curriculum by content is not inevitable. Bodies such as the Council for National Academic Awards and, before its demise, the University Grants Committee have repeatedly in science subject reviews expressed concern at the domination of curricula by factual content. Professional bodies such as the Institute of Physics, the London Mathematical Society and the Royal Society for Chemistry are examining the question and finding that much of what one department finds essential is not taught, let alone learnt, in an apparently very similar department offering the same qualification. For example, it appears that the common content of honours chemistry degrees in UK universities amounts to no more than 30 per cent of what is taught in any one of them.

The differences in curricula are particularly notable in later years. For example, there is much similarity across English mathematics degree courses for the first year and a half but, overall, it seems that there is little consensus on what is 'essential', with much depending on the particular bias of the department.

Certainly the difficulties should not be underestimated. Science and mathematics do require a solid base on which to build. Much of science requires a solid basis of mathematics. This inevitably makes special demands on the non-traditionally qualified applicant.

Strategies for moving forward

What is important is that the difficulties are not seen as insuperable. In future, the differences between students – now called 'non-traditional' and 'traditional' – will become less pronounced. Departments will continue to recruit from schools where, through GCSE and SCE, BTEC and SCOTVEC, there are significant shifts away from the conventional 'academic' approach of A levels and Highers, but they must also recruit an increasing number of mature students lacking standard qualifications. Further challenges will be posed by the greater movement of students across the European Community and between and within institutions, with the growth of credit accumulation and transfer. Fresh thinking is needed about what is to be learnt and why.

The assumption, generally implicit in many curricula, that the majority of science and mathematics graduates go on to become scientists or mathematicians, is increasingly being recognized as false. The majority, even of 'good' graduates, do not. Science and mathematics graduates go to a wide range of jobs. Even those who go into research typically use only a small proportion of the content conventionally seen as being so essential to their courses.

Employers too often find graduates lacking in problem-solving skills and unable to communicate accurately and effectively orally or in writing.

The 'fitness for purpose' view of quality in the teaching and learning of science and mathematics must be taken seriously. We must think less in terms of the vocational needs of the training of research scientists and more of the general needs of employment and the broader development opportunities that can be offered by a scientific training.

Perhaps the position of science and mathematics as neither essentially vocational like medicine nor essentially non-vocational like the humanities lies at the root of the misconceived view that there are special difficulties in introducing the development of capability through science and mathematics higher education. Yet there is much in conventional science and mathematics courses which can be built on. It is common for courses to include a major research project in the final year. Where this is the case, it is often observed that the rate of development of students undertaking such a project far outstrips that in earlier years. Increasingly, projects involve employers as external collaborators rather than being exclusively dependent on staff academic and research interests.

Understanding, communication skills, problem-solving skills all rapidly develop within the context of such activity. The student shares responsibility for negotiating the project objectives with academic staff and any external collaborators. Project work can be introduced into earlier years of courses with similar benefits.

It is also being recognized that the traditional activity of students working in pairs in laboratories in the sciences and mathematics can be turned into group work with very little adjustment. Increasing group size and providing less structured experiments can help students to learn more explicitly about working in groups, leadership, communication, the use of critical analysis and judgement, and interpersonal skills development. This can involve learning contracts, self- and peer-group assessment, and encounters with unfamiliar problems that stimulate creativity and active inquiry skills.

Option courses, choices of experiments in laboratories and case studies allow students to specialize within a subject while forming a ready basis for their playing a role in negotiating learning goals and outcomes. Without denying the need for a 'core' of necessary skills and fundamental knowledge, this process of negotiation can be begun much earlier in courses than is usual, giving students a sense of ownership over their learning from the outset.

Where it is possible, the introduction of work placements into the early years can give those with no work experience a context in which to set their learning. Such opportunities also allow those with previous work experience to build on that in ways that enhance motivation and involvement, as well as the understanding of core principles and pertinent theory. A period in another country provides similar benefits. Such activities may not have immediate vocational pay-off, but contribute to the broader development of future scientists and mathematicians.

First year courses and pre-first year courses which develop scientific and mathematical skills, knowledge and understanding through a capability approach can considerably even things up for mature students with their greater life experience. These initiatives also provide a more rewarding educational experience for the conventional entrant.

Such strategies can change the image of science and mathematics, and so help to attract and retain conventional and non-conventional entrants. Given the current financial cost to an institution of losing students in mathematics and sciences, these considerations will continue to be especially important if resources further diminish.

The introduction of capability principles and practices into science and mathematics courses in higher education must be taken through to assessment. It is not viable to expect students to work to develop skills and understanding which are not given full credit through assessment.

We cannot expect to introduce the development of capability into the curriculum if in assessment we fall back on assessing rote learning of factual content. The introduction of capability concepts will normally involve introducing a substantial element of in-course assessment. The value of self-assessment and peer-assessment is also becoming recognized. The opportunities offered by assessment for enhancing student involvement, motivation and the quality of their learning are considerable.

Below we describe a few examples of the capability approach which are currently working. Although we discuss them under the four Higher Education for Capability themes, it will be obvious that each example embodies more than one of the themes.

Theme One: Reviewing and building on experience
In science and mathematics there have been various attempts to respond to the greater diversity of intake. Perhaps because of the nature of the subjects there has been less straightforward building on life and employment experience. However, efforts are made to enable students to see the links between science and mathematics and their own experience. The more usual approach is to provide a non-traditional start to a course where capability skills are strongly emphasized, leading students towards the more technical aspects which are taught by more conventional means.

The Polytechnic of East London {43} runs a HITECC foundation programme for students wishing to enter mathematics, science, engineering or technology. It is a one-year full-time (or equivalent) programme offered by the Continuing Education Department, a central services unit co-operating with all teaching departments. The underpinning learning philosophy is that excellence in knowledge acquisition and skills of analysis can be achieved only if capability skills are developed as an integral part of the subject.

The first six weeks of the course are spent in training and development in capability skills so that students have the tools to develop a capability perspective in their later studies and to take responsibility for their own learning. Skills which are developed include study-time management, organizing, decision making and oral and written communication, together with interpersonal leadership and team membership skills. Study methods include individual and group work, non-directed private study, practice in using resource-based learning, case studies, simulations and closed circuit television.

This initial development of capability skills is followed by three further components: core mathematics and science; new technology appreciation; and a specialist study in mathematics, a science or an area of engineering. The programme content is student derived and managed. Students profile themselves, plan personal development paths and goals, and demonstrate their achievement through negotiated in-course assessment and final assessment in the form of a portfolio. Students can choose a recommended core content providing the prerequisite knowledge and skills required for any one of the 26 undergraduate courses to which the programme is linked.

The training in capability skills comes at the beginning of the course so that students are enabled to manage their learning more effectively and to integrate capability skills into their knowledge acquisition. The core mathematics and science component, as well as the development of technical skills and knowledge, encourages further skills of personal organization and time management through self-paced and self-managed resource-based learning. Students also develop an ability to work without supervision. The new technology appreciation component helps to integrate the course with a student's life experience. The specialist study component has students working largely without supervision in a specialist teaching department, further developing self-reliance and confidence through working on projects and using specialist learning resources.

Approximately 25 per cent of the course specifically covers general capability development and this is reflected in the balance of assessment; however, the capability skills acquired underpin learning throughout the course. Excellence of knowledge acquisition and skills of analysis are assessed in all four components through the application of theory to practical situations and life examples. Breadth and depth of knowledge are not considered to be as important as the demonstration of understanding of the subject, its application and relevance to work and life.

This emphasis helps non-traditional entrants to bring some of their previous experience into their learning and so gain confidence. It provides an opportunity for converters, the unemployed and women returners, for example, to enter mathematics and science. Students who take the course are better prepared to manage the remainder of their undergraduate studies. At the Polytechnic of East London the course operates as a foundation programme. However, many features of the approach, in particular the initial component developing capability skills, could be taken into a three-year degree programme with great benefit to the learning throughout the remainder of the undergraduate programme.

A similar approach is adopted in the first year chemistry course in the Department of Applied Chemistry and Life Sciences in the Polytechnic of North London {145}. In the first seven weeks of the course there are no lectures. Students are invited to learn by addressing a number of questions. The material on which the questions are based is covered by set books so students have easy access to the information required for formulating answers. Negotiated targets are set for students.

The students' study is supported by tutorials where the emphasis is on student participation. The better prepared students produce high quality work in good depth; they are also generally very supportive to students with a weaker background, enabling these students to progress more rapidly and to tackle their learning in a far more effective way than would be possible if they were trying to learn on their own from lecture notes. The students with the stronger background move rapidly through the material they have already encountered and have greater opportunity to study more advanced material. Students are able to set their own pace.

Progress tests are used to inform students of their areas of strength and weakness and students can return to areas where further work is shown to be necessary.

After the first seven weeks, the remainder of the course is taught in a more traditional way through lectures and tutorials but there is still a component of self-learning material to support and reinforce the learning habits developed in the first seven weeks.

Later in the year, a programme of guest speakers is organized. They talk on important topics of the day, for example, chemistry and the environment or the place of the pharmaceutical industry in society. On the basis of these keynote speeches students develop their own talks on a theme of their choice. The talks are delivered to their fellow students and a written resumé is produced. The majority of students are highly motivated by this, often seeing for the first time the interconnection between science, society and themselves. The students invariably produce well-researched work.

Theme Two: Planning, negotiation and approval
Examples of student negotiation and planning of their own learning in mathematics and science appear to be less extensive than in other subject areas. Perhaps this is because there is a conviction that there is an

essential body of knowledge and skills which students must acquire, and that it is the teacher who is uniquely placed to define what should be learnt. However, in some courses there is a degree of negotiation, particularly on the rate of learning, but this can extend further. This is demonstrated by the above examples.

As noted above, in the HITECC programme at the Polytechnic of East London {43}, the form of both in-course assessment and final assessment is the subject of student negotiation and this allows students to plan their personal development paths and goals. In the example from the Polytechnic of North London, the targets set for students are the subject of negotiation and this allows students to move through the material at a pace which reflects their backgrounds and preparation.

In an interesting course which has been operating for the past three years in the Department of Applied Sciences at Staffordshire Polytechnic {203}, science students and art students with a graphic design background are put into a customer/client relationship. The task is the development of a set of laboratory-safety videos and posters aimed specifically at young technicians. The science students work on the message and specification and negotiate the production with design students, with the academic staff remaining very much at the periphery.

There is great scope for such cross-subject projects involving interdisciplinary teamwork. As well as fostering negotiation and planning between student groups, they strengthen teamwork, communication and interpersonal skills and provide an insight into another subject discipline.

Theme Three: Active and interactive learning

There are a number of examples of the introduction of active learning methods into mathematics and science. This is perhaps because there is a well established tradition of final year research project work. It is increasingly becoming accepted that the learning advantages which come from these projects can also be gained through project work at all stages of a degree programme.

For example, at the University of Leicester {110}, in the Department of Chemistry, first year students are offered a choice from a range of approximately 30 projects in physical chemistry. Many of the projects require the use of sophisticated research apparatus. Each project involves making quantitative measurements and is designed to illustrate a key idea in modern physical chemistry. All are open ended.

Students tackle the projects in small teams. They are advised to spend the first week planning the project and assigning responsibilities and duties to members of the team. This develops students' planning and team-working skills. The second and third weeks are spent carrying out the project. Although demonstrators are on hand, the students are encouraged to organize their own time. This develops leadership, self-organization and teamwork skills.

The fourth week is spent discussing results and preparing reports. Students help and teach one another as they argue through their experimental results. Each team produces a written report and a synopsis of the report which is displayed in the department. In addition, each team presents its results in a seminar chaired by a member of staff. All first year students attend the seminar and all other members of the department, staff and students, are invited to attend. Each member of the first year assesses each project with particular reference to communication and presentation. This assessment is combined with another given by a member of staff to provide an overall assessment.

Students enjoy the team projects and appear to get a great deal from them. One student commented that for the first time she felt she was a real chemist, doing real experiments – not just routine experiments with well-established results – looking up original and 'proper' papers in the library, and talking to other chemists about what she had discovered.

The School of Applied Sciences at Wolverhampton Polytechnic {251} offers a module through which students develop and organize a control campaign in some area of medical or veterinary parasitology. The module is available to second and third year students. The scheme gives all responsibility for researching relevant information, synthesizing a feasible solution and designing the campaign materials to the students. Input from the lecturer is confined to encouragement and advice rather than supervision. The students work in groups and so develop the skills of defining group objectives, assigning tasks and reporting back and, thereby, the skills of relating to others in the group, such as listening, arguing a case and accepting criticism.

Students agree a particular parasitological problem with the course tutors. They then determine the target of the campaign – for example, health workers, veterinarians, the general public, teachers, pet owners, livestock owners, etc – and the format of the campaign. The campaigns are based in an environment with which the students are familiar.

This approach allows the normal academic process of learning the symptoms and cures for a disease to be extended to include the practical application of this knowledge. Students are thereby introduced to the problems encountered in applying scientific data to a specific problem.

They learn by experience which data are essential and hence to be selective in the knowledge they acquire.

Students submit a rating of the performance of the contribution made by each of the other students in the group. These are averaged out and the mark awarded to the group by staff members is divided between the students according to this. Each student is also asked to produce a short report on their own development of capability skills and to comment on the project. In the main, students enjoy working on the project. They recognize that it improves their capability skills, notably in communication and group working and that it involves solving a real problem.

Theme Four: Assessment

Assessment in mathematics and science has traditionally been rooted in the three-hour examination with little, if any, weight given to in-course assessment. Even in the laboratory-based sciences, assessment of laboratory work has, surprisingly, usually made little contribution to final assessment. However, the examples suggest that attitudes to assessment are changing.

In first year of the BSc/BSc (Hons) in Mathematical Sciences in the Department of Mathematics and Statistics at Paisley College {159}, a 'mathematical sciences laboratory' has been established as a compulsory component of the course. A series of case studies is assigned to students. Students work on these in teams of three. They receive a problem, stated in non-mathematical terms, and are required to use mathematical methods and a computer to find a solution, finally producing a group report which describes the mathematical content used, together with an account of the group's solution, stated in non-mathematical terms. Each group of students is responsible for the organization of its own work, in terms of discussing solution strategies, assigning among the members of the group responsibilities for carrying out investigations and experiments involving computer packages, and the production of the group's report, for which the use of a word-processor is encouraged.

The mathematical sciences laboratory work is judged completely through in-course assessment. This is based on individual laboratory reports and on the group study reports. Marks are awarded for quality of presentation as well as for mathematical content. This assessment contributes 30 per cent of the mark for the first year mathematical sciences course.

Problems with this type of assessment have emerged. Some students feel that marking is not uniform. It has proved difficult to eliminate this perception as some tutors inevitably give more help than others, meaning that similar reports can merit different marks from different tutors. A partial solution has been to make detailed marking schemes available to tutors. Also, resentments can surface in certain groups in which some students contribute more than others. In such cases the solution has been for the group to negotiate with the tutor a weighting arrangement, whereby different members of the group receive different proportions of the marks.

The approach has proved popular with students and with employers. It has been particularly beneficial to students who were previously perceived to be weak in mathematics.

The School of Health Sciences at Wolverhampton Polytechnic {253} runs a final year module in Applied Pharmacology and Toxicology. During the second half of the final semester, students undertake a special project using a combination of computer simulations and working as a project team to produce a pharmacodynamic and pharmacokinetic report on a range of drugs. Students work in groups and are required to produce a report of not more than 3000 words. The report is also presented orally to all students on the course with a time allowance of 30 minutes for presentation and 10 minutes for discussion. No credit is given for the oral presentation if the reports are simply read.

The project is assessed by a mixture of tutor assessment, intra-group assessment and inter-group assessment. The mark from the project contributes 50 per cent to the overall practical assessment of the course. The group report is assessed by all staff teaching the module and the mark given for the report is allocated to each individual member of the group. In the intra-group assessment, each member of the group assesses each other member's performance and contribution to the work. In the inter-group assessment, each group assesses the performance of the other groups in the oral presentation of the report. The group presentations are also assessed by the teaching staff. The overall assessment of the project is divided into 30 per cent for the staff-assessed group report, 30 per cent for intra-group assessment, 20 per cent for inter-group assessment and 20 per cent for the staff-assessed group presentation.

Conclusion

Much is happening. As the examples above show, capability ideas *are* being introduced into higher education courses in the sciences and mathematics, though not always under that name: sometimes as enterprise, sometimes as transferable skills, common skills, or competences, and often under no banner at all but in response to the diverse needs of students as identified by themselves, by staff or by external organizations. But more is needed.

The introduction of capability or other student-centred approaches does not offer science and mathematics higher education on the cheap. The opposite is likely to be the case. High-quality education, whatever the level, does not come cheap. Adequate provision of resources in mathematics and sciences is essential. Quality and capability are not consistent with the 'teach 'em cheap, stack 'em deep' philosophy of education. There is, however, tremendous scope for re-thinking the use of existing resources to alternative ends, as evidenced by work in this volume.

Scientific education in future will need to place value on creative and active inquiry, on awareness of oneself and of one's world, on working with others, and on continuous learning and development, as well as on the acquisition of specialist understanding and skills. The challenge is not only to develop scientists and mathematicians, but to develop people with a scientific or mathematical education who can live and work in a rapidly changing world. There can be little doubt that graduates who combine technical subject-based skills and knowledge with capability skills are what the nation needs and what employers are increasingly demanding.

Reference

ACOST (1991) *Science and Technology: Education and Employment*. HMSO.

Chapter Eight
Capability Through Teacher Education

Susan Weil and David Bridges

Introduction

Teacher education: change at the interface of three systems

Teacher educators work at the interface of three systems, each of which is undergoing profound and rapid change, to the point that, as Charles Handy puts it, it becomes almost 'discontinuous' (Handy, 1989). The enormous changes in curriculum, pedagogy and assessment in the school system for which teacher educators are preparing their students have presented them with a number of challenges:

- teacher educators themselves have had to face the challenge of keeping their own knowledge and experience up to date;
- they have had to revise their own approaches to teacher education, to reflect the changes which have taken place and continue to take place in the school curriculum;
- they have had to equip their students to handle the changing pedagogy of schools, with increasing emphasis on experiential learning, collaborative group projects, and self-assessment; and
- they have had to begin to respond to the changing experiences of teaching, learning and curriculum which students at initial and post-experience levels are beginning to bring with them into higher education.

Dramatic and continuing changes in higher education are requiring teacher educators to respond a whole new agenda of issues including:

- an expanding student population (approaching a 30 per cent increase in teacher training between 1985 and 1990);
- higher expectations of 'cost effectiveness' – which means among other things that the expected expansion in student numbers is being accom-

modated, and will continue to be accommodated, without anything
like a corresponding increase in staff resources;

- tighter external auditing and accountability, increasingly articulated
  in the language of 'quality control' and designed to ensure that those
  responsible directly or indirectly for funding get what they want (eg,
  what is expressed in the Secretary of State's criteria mediated through
  the Committee for the Accreditation of Teacher Education or (CATE)
  rather than what HE institutions might independently seek to provide);
- increased dependency of institutions on their capacity to attract income from a variety of clients – students with their purses full of fees
  (or half full of borrowed money) form the central but by no means
  only group – a pressure which has prompted the development of a
  wide range of client-centred strategies, including investment in out-
  reach courses, marketing and publicity, negotiation of tailor-made
  training programmes and packages, consumer research, etc; and
- ambivalence in the polytechnic sector as to whether schools or departments of education should be trying rapidly to establish a substantial
  research role and uncertainty in the university sector as to the extent
  to which particular departments will continue to be funded in support
  of such a role.

At the same time, and partly as a consequence of these developments
teacher educators are having to respond to change in their client groups.

Not only is the student population growing, it is also changing in
character. The incessant demand for more teachers forces the profession
to look for recruits from different populations than those that have
traditionally entered teaching. But combined with this has been a growing recognition that there are sections of the population with a rich
contribution to make to teaching which has not previously been properly
acknowledged – this includes people whom the system has previously
worked to discourage from entry into teaching, such as students from
British ethnic minority groups, people who have not followed conventional educational patterns of progress and qualification, people who
have already developed the beginnings of a career in some other walk of
life and people who have taken time out of teaching to bring up a family.

Increasingly teacher education institutions have been developing
systems and courses designed to enable these groups to enter or re-enter
teaching or perhaps to retrain for a different age range or specialism. But
their needs are not the same as the traditional postgraduate student
straight from university or the BEd student who has arrived at college
straight from school. Nor indeed are they the same as each other. And
teacher education institutions have had to adapt and are continuing to

learn to adapt their approaches to this new population. The accreditation of prior learning and achievement, and the development of unit/credit frameworks are but two examples of responses to change now in evidence.

In the in-service field, of course, teacher education institutions are having to adjust to the major shift in the dispersal of resources and power – in particular the dispersal of resources for in-service training – from a relatively small number of Local Education Authorities across a very large number of schools. What kind of arrangements will allow teacher education institutions to negotiate cost-effective packages which will meet the needs of such a large number of clients remains to be seen.

Finally many teacher institutions are finding too that there are other clients, in public service organizations and in industry, who recognize and welcome the professional skills which teacher educators have to offer, and these are opening new and challenging opportunities for diversification.

The response in teacher education

Somewhere at the interface of these changing systems is a force of teacher educators seeking to survive or, indeed, more ambitiously, seeking to rise to Peters' (1987) image and aspiration of 'thriving on chaos'. Some of these have found support in effective new alliances (eg, the strong links between a teacher education institution, an LEA and schools reflected in the Oxford internship scheme) or in collaborations between teacher education institutions (eg, the Eastern Region Teacher Education Consortium). Some have been supported in the process of adapting to change by major projects like the Department of Employment Enterprise in Higher Education initiative, the Enterprise Awareness and Teacher Education initiative, which is now also located within the Department of Employment, and the Higher Education for Capability Project sponsored by the RSA.

The notion of capability, though not necessarily in exactly the same language, runs through all these initiatives. While it would be absurd to pretend that it was some magical incantation which would instantly quieten all the storms which buffet teacher education , it is nevertheless a notion which wraps up an interconnected set of responses to some of the issues raised by the changing educational environment.

What is just as important, if not more so, is that the kind of principles articulated in terms of capability are consonant with and, arguably, express in the language of the 1990s, the underlying educational commitments which have perhaps characterized teacher education institutions for the last quarter of a century at least. We refer to a commitment to:

- the development of the students'/teachers' independence and autonomy, including their capacity to be agents of their own learning;
- the development of their own practical and creative capacity to make things happen; and
- the development of their sense of, and willingness to accept, responsibility, and a recognition that with that go obligations of accountability.

This much, we suggest, is firmly within the established tradition of the basic values which underpin teacher education. What is perhaps innovative in the education for capability movement is, in general terms, the application of these kind of principles to the changing environment of the late twentieth century and, more specifically, a particular emphasis on the conditions under which (student) teachers develop not merely the capacity to decide what they should do – in their own lives and careers or in their classrooms – but the *capability* to act in and upon a world teeming with people with competing as well as complementary aspirations, who are as likely to be hostile to as supportive of their achievement.

As in other chapters of this book, we are organizing our exploration and exemplification of capability principles in practice in four sections. Not all of the examples provided illustrate unqualified success. This would in any case be fairly implausible. What they do illustrate is how teacher education institutions are combining, in a variety of ways:

- a student centredness which is deeply rooted in the traditions of teacher education;
- an attempt to equip students with the kind of flexibility, independence or capability which will enable them to cope with an environment of discontinuous change; and
- a client orientation which is demanded by the increasingly market-driven character of educational provision.

These represent, of course, some rather different principles but it is often difficult to separate them in the day-to-day life of higher education, and their practical consequences may not be wholly dissimilar.

Theme One: Reviewing and building on experience
The development through the 1970s and 1980s of in-service training for teachers brought home firmly some new lessons to those responsible,

namely that they were teaching people who could and should contribute substantially to each other's learning from the wealth of prior and continuing experience of teaching which they brought with them. Approaches to training were developed which relied heavily on teachers acting, for example, as researchers in their own classrooms or working together in collaborative groups to share and analyse experience.

Such developments have perhaps been less evident in BEd and PGCE programmes, but as the students entering these courses become noticeably more mature (several PGCE tutors report an average age of 27 or over in their groups), they bring with them increasingly rich and diverse experience of parenting, working and caring for young and old, and their own experience as learners in schools and colleges.

These students are increasingly bringing with them, too, experience in schools and higher education institutions of more comprehensive forms of recognition of their learning and achievement (eg, in school records of achievement) and more flexible forms of accreditation of learning (eg, in the acceptance of project presentations, or of courses taken abroad, as components of a degree).

Teacher educators are increasingly challenged therefore to recognize (in the curriculum they offer as well as in assessment), to value and to accredit a variety of experience which students have acquired prior to entry on their course or which they continue to gain in parallel with their course.

It is quite clear moreover that this expectation will rise as, for example, the requirements for the award of qualified teacher status come increasingly to be articulated in terms of demonstrated competence rather than in terms of specific programmes of study undertaken. Now that the principle has been accepted that one may come to have and to show the required competence (or, more typically, competences) through a variety of routes, it is a small step to acknowledging that it may equally be derived from prior or continuing experience outside any programme study.

Among the submissions received, this theme was well-illustrated in the context of in-service training, but the dearth of examples from initial training may suggest that, if the above analysis is correct, this sector has some way to go before it is responsive to the changing environment which is identified.

Profiling as strategy for recognizing pre- and post-course experience
At the University of Cambridge Department of Education, teachers on the PGCE course {23} have been involved in a pilot scheme that builds

actively on student interests by involving them in planning for and
compiling a 'record of achievement' (57 Participated in 1989/1990; 200
in 1990/1991). This seeks to promote student autonomy by involving
them in identifying the teaching competences they will develop during
the course, and planning for learning. Each student, in consultation with
the trainers, identifies the skills and knowledge he/she should acquire
and the ways in which the various elements in the course will serve those
training needs. The record provides a vehicle for discussion and feedback, and a framework for noting progress and building confidence. The
whole record is designed with a view to it being of use in the following
year when the new teacher is in his/her first teaching post. It thus
generates a language for exploring and building on experience and
interests prior to the PGCE, as well as learning gained through the course
itself.

At present, the record serves as a documentation of formative assessment, in which self-assessment plays a key role. It records progress, and
is updated on several occasions during the training year. The record does
not however contribute to the final qualification. This decision was under
review at the time of the submission.

The six aims of the scheme are as follows:

(1) *A record of training* – to provide a unified approach and the opportunity for each student to compile a record of training, experience,
achievement, competences and training needs, and to make the learning aims more explicit by incorporating in this record a list of teaching
competences.

(2) *A tool for student development* – to support student learning by making
profiling part of the learning process, to improve feedback to students,
and to encourage student autonomy.

(3) *Partnership with schools* – to improve communication between the
department and teacher supervisors by beginning the developments,
in partnership with them, of an agreed framework both for advising
students during their training and for assessment and reporting at the
end of each phase of training.

(4) *Helping students to become reflective practitioners* – to raise student
awareness, to train them in self-evaluation and to give students an
experience which will be helpful if they have to deal with records of
achievement in schools and undergo teacher appraisal.

(5) *Applying for the first teaching post* – to enable students to provide at
interview, if requested, a full record of what they can do.

(6) *A bridge to the induction year* – to enable the student to compile a list
of future training needs and a full record of what has been achieved

and can be done as a result of the PGCE course so as to inform and guide the support to be given to the new teacher in a first post. {23}

The development work entailed in introducing such a scheme has been undertaken by department members as part of their normal teaching commitment.

Extra resources have been minimal... We have applied for research funding as part of a proposal relating to teacher education nationally and the variety of routes into the profession but with no success so far. {23}

This has resulted in some critical decisions about when and how individual time can be offered to students.

It has therefore not been possible to give staff the time for interviewing individual students which would have been desirable. Most of the personal guidance has had to take place either as part of normal group work or on a one-to-one basis during the regular teaching sessions, with private interviews during teaching practice and on two or three other occasions during the year. {23}

The pressure of time, combined with the conservatism of some colleagues, has resulted in this development being experienced by students as bolted on, rather than as something integrally related to the examination on which the final qualification depends.

For profiling to be given the importance to make it effective, it must be a course requirement. It cannot wholly succeed as an 'add-on'. {23}

As confidence and experience builds, various strategies are being used to win support, such as consultation, ongoing discussion and a professionally evaluated pilot programme. In addition, the benefits to students become increasingly evident as time progresses.

In addition to those mentioned, it sets the agenda for training, raises awareness of the range of knowledge, understanding and skills required, increases feedback, informs choices, generally encourages and promotes confidence... It also aids communication between the department and schools. Consultation with teachers helps sustain partnership. {23}

One of the main outcomes of the evaluation of the first version of the profile was a recognition that the department had attempted to profile far too many competences. Apart from making the task almost impracticable it made it impossible to explore areas of competency seriously. The next version of the profile will reduce the number of competences to be assessed to six or eight. (Copies of the evaluation report are available from the department.)

Accrediting academic development and experience

At the Polytechnic of Wales, academic staff have the opportunity of taking a Postgraduate Certificate in Teaching and Learning {221} based on capability principles and practices. The programme enables staff members to build a programme based entirely on problems and questions arising out of their own experiences as teachers. The pace and style of learning is entirely determined by the individual staff members. Content is negotiated as relevant to needs and interests arising from the academic's own work. Completion is based on five units, each representing 70 hours of work, the majority of which is time already spent in preparation and teaching. There are three core units, and two additional units, the content and process of which build entirely on participants' experience and interest through negotiation with mentors. The remaining time is spent putting together evidence for the assessment of self-selected teaching/learning developments.

Increasingly, access and other changes are placing new demands on academic staff to develop new understandings of teaching/ learning and assessment. Academics are able to enter HE teaching without prior qualifications preparing them for that role and function. Although this remains the case, as academics develop in response to new demands, a growing concern is whether and how to accredit such learning. This example signals a direction that may become more and more at issue within not only in the training of academics, but also in teacher training more generally, if greater emphasis is to be placed on in-school development.

This particular initiative arose out of the enthusiasm of staff in the Teaching Development Group who had set out to address the limitations of existing provision.

Existing external provision for in-service certification tended to have only limited relevance to the day-to-day work of staff. It also required them to spend considerable time away from their duties. It was decided to develop a certificate programme that was wholly relevant to the development of teaching and learning processes, with work taking place on an action research basis underpinned by resource materials to provide the necessary theoretical basis. {221}

The following key features of the course design were intended to maximize opportunities for flexibility, relevance, challenge and support.

- *Flexible learning approach:* participants work at their own pace, in their own way, using resource materials made available.
- *Negotiated learning agreements:* participants decide what they want to do, how they want to do it, and when they want to complete it by, as a basis for a negotiated agreement between yourself and the Programme Board of Studies.
- *Total relevance to your normal work:* all the work in the negotiated agreement is intended to be directly relevant to participants' teaching. Thus, there are no artificial hoops to jump through.
- *Mentor support:* to help participants implement their negotiated agreement, they have two mentors – one from the programme and one from their own department.
- *Self- and peer-assessment:* participants design their own assessment criteria as part of their negotiated learning agreement and the success of their work is judged on these criteria, by themselves and their peers.
- *Credit rated professional development:* each programme is accredited on the polytechnic's Credit Accumulation scheme and will count towards the award of the certificate. {221}

This programme places a high premium on learner responsibility that builds on prior interests and experiences. Content coverage is intended to be related to academics' own learning goals and is negotiated in terms of what is perceived to be relevant to personal/professional concerns and interests. Nonetheless this programme illustrates how accountability can be married to learner responsibility to meet the requirements of the certificate. Each candidate is required to have carried out some work in each of the following areas.

- Developing and employing a system of student self-assessment and/or peer-assessment in an agreed part of the curriculum and evaluating the learning outcomes of such assessment.
- Designing, piloting, and evaluating a short open or flexible learning package for the delivery of an agreed part of the curriculum.
- Producing evidence to demonstrate a range of teaching competences, such as giving large and small group presentations and facilitating tutorials, workshops, seminars and practical work. {221}

A great deal of flexibility is thus possible within the development of the learning agreement.

Theme Two: Planning, negotiation and approval

As with our previous theme, there are more ready examples of developments of this kind within the in-service than the pre-service context. This is partly because the content and methods of delivery of initial training by higher education institutions are defined with ever increasing specificity by the Secretary of State who makes conformity with his specification a condition of course accreditation. A national curriculum for teacher education (which may well include the early stages of in-service training as well as pre-service training) cannot be far away. In these circumstances there is limited scope for flexibility on the part of either trainers or trainees.

There is nevertheless always some scope for negotiation and the exercise of choice and the principle of a contract which sets out the obligations of students and tutors to each other is arguably a fruitful one. It establishes education and training as an activity governed by publicly accessible rules and reciprocal rights and duties, an activity in which both students and tutors have responsibility and accountability.

Negotiating and contracting an Education Unit in a BEd (Hons)
At Sheffield City Polytechnic, 200 second year BEd {181} students on the primary and secondary courses complete a total of twelve 40-hour units of study/work per year. One unit is devoted to the theoretical aspects of education. This is completed by means of negotiated contracts, the outcomes of which are in turn presented to tutorial groups of about 20 students. The content of the syllabus is divided into three or four themes. Students arrange themselves in groups of four and negotiate with their education tutor a total of three or four contracts, one relating to each of the content themes. Their aim is to fulfil the degree requirements as specified in the submission to CNAA of which they are given a copy. They are encouraged to negotiate their contracts so that they can fulfil them in ways that best fit their personal interests and needs, strengths and weaknesses. Each contract takes approximately four to six weeks to negotiate, implement and present. The form of presentations is up to students and tutors, with encouragement for a wide variety of approaches (eg, audio-tape, video, oral, written, visual, etc). Tutors support students through keynote and explanatory lectures, workshops and meetings with each contract group.

The unit has so far been assessed by summative assignment. This has to be carefully designed to take account of the particular style of teaching and learning.

The tutors' decision to introduce a capability-type approach to a compulsory year two unit on theoretical aspects of education (40 hours of educational studies) with 200 students arose out of a number of concerns, including:

- the increasing diversity in the student population, in which groups varied in terms of their academic background, their experience with children and their development of skills relevant to teaching (such as communication and teamwork);
- student needs for opportunities to develop specific skills and their overall capability for living, as well as for working, as a teacher;
- student needs to be motivated if they were to benefit from the theoretical knowledge demanded by course syllabus requirements, as validated by CNAA;
- the marginalization of education studies in the BEd degree as a consequence of the priority given by CATE demands for school experience, subject content programmes and subject methodology; and
- the desire to enable the growing numbers of mature women students to work where, when and in which style they prefer, coupled with a belief that traditional higher education teaching methods did not address these equal opportunities issues. {181}

These concerns were combined with the tutors' values about what kind of education develops more effective teachers. They were also influenced by tutors' personal and professional backgrounds. The latter made them predisposed to student-centred and capability approaches, with an overall concern for equal opportunities:

In particular, this development has made it easier for mature women students to cope with all the commitments that this implies... We feel that this system addresses the issue of equal opportunities far more successfully than the traditional higher education teaching methods often used. {181}

The overall emphasis of the course is on teaching and learning processes and their management. The thematic areas for which students would be both responsible and accountable through negotiation of learning contracts were:

- The Developing Person;
- Understanding Learning;
- Social Context of Child Development. {181}

In addition, a contract approach is related to the term of teaching practice.

The responsibilities of students and tutors are clearly spelled out in the course booklet. For example:

Responsibility of students
- Read all materials distributed by the course tutor.
- Play an active part in the negotiation, implementation and presentation of the contract.
- Ensure that his/her work and understanding are of an appropriate academic standard: this involves paying attention to the feedback given by the tutor and other members of the group.
- Allocate time for reading and related activities so that the requirements of CNAA are fulfilled.
- Negotiate with the group individual responsibilities in the completion of the contract.
- Present himself/herself at times agreed by both the tutor and other members of the contract group.
- Be required to fulfil these responsibilities conscientiously and to the best of his/her abilities.
- Involve himself/herself honestly and constructively in self- and group-appraisal of each contract.

Responsibility of tutors
- Be available at designated rooms at designated times and only those times.
- Negotiate and approve the contracts and direct the processes by which these are achieved.
- Ensure that the package of contracts fulfils the aims of the second year course.
- Inform students where to obtain appropriate source material, additional to the list of references provided.
- Give regular feedback and guidance which will enable students to be assured that the work they are doing is of an appropriate academic standard.
- Monitor the progress of each contract and, as part of this, explain and expand on any of the content areas outlined in the list of materials to be studied without removing from the student the principal responsibility for his/her learning. {181}

When the course team introduced this development, they were working within a number of constraints. The rationale, aims, content and assessment of the course had been agreed by CNAA two years previously. Their commitment to the use of negotiated learning, and the use of learning contracts, had to be worked through within this pre-existing framework. Staff also have to meet frequently to plan, discuss and give each other support, as there is no institutional staff development or support for this kind of initiative.

> The only real obstacle was fear – that of tutors, who were afraid that they were abnegating their duties, and that of students afraid of responsibility. This is a constant fear and we live with it and overcome it by supporting and encouraging each other. The teaching team is strong and closely knit and has been able, so far, to absorb and help newcomers. Students get our support and each other's support. {181}

Reservations are gradually being dropped as staff and students gain experience of the programme and its benefits. Evaluations by tutors and students, and a small-scale piece of research undertaken by a colleague in another department have pointed to the following specific gains:

> ...improved study skills, higher motivation, much greater understanding than when we used traditional teaching methods, more reading done, a high quality of presentations, increased student autonomy and improved abilities to work at their own pace in their chosen environment, to negotiate and to work in teams. In addition, the initiative has refreshed tutor morale and communication. {181}

The last point is frequently reported, despite the fact that often such developments are initiated on the backs of traditional programmes at the expense of the individual tutors' publications, research, and personal life. At a time when morale in higher education is low, managers need to consider how they can stimulate and support such innovations across an institution, through their managerial and leadership style, and the structures and processes of the institution.

Negotiating on the edges of traditional programmes
At the University of Warwick {230}, students on the BA with Qualified Teacher Status take a course called 'Lifelong Learning and the School Curriculum'. This makes up one quarter of their final year's work and spans 25 teaching weeks. The course lecturers have introduced informal

processes of negotiating and contracting into this quite traditional programme. The course is scheduled for one lecture hour plus two seminar
hours per week, with five revision weeks in the third term. This course
is assessed by 3000 words of course work as well as a three-hour
examination.

The introduction of informal processes of negotiating and contracting
can be a daunting task, if they are introduced in the final year for the first
time and go against the culture of the course as a whole. On this
programme, course tutors do this firstly in the seminars.

> The purposes and broad areas of knowledge relevant to the theme are
> sketched. Students are invited to write, then discuss and pool, their expec-
> tations, etc.
>   The programme of activities through the year is partly prefigured and
> partly negotiated, with the examination reflecting the areas of focus rather
> than dictating a syllabus. {230}

Experiential activities also promote more active responsible learning, out
of which such negotiations can spring more naturally.

> Structured experiential learning situations encourage students to reflect
> actively on recollections of their school days, their teaching practice ex-
> perience and experience as university students over the four years of the
> course. The immediate experience of the course and the group is also treated
> as relevant learning data; reflexivity is fostered. {230}

In this way, the values of reflexivity and of prior and immediate experience as 'learning data' are reinforced. Students are thus taking responsibility for working with their own experience, and learning how to learn
from it. Students also take responsibility, individually and in groups, for
other forms of field work and data collection, in relation to questions
they have identified as important to their own development as teachers
and in relation to the theme of this course.

This shift towards more active responsible learning on the part of
students represented a first step both for the lecturers and the students.
In the tutor's words, course membership took 'half a term to stabilize as
the word got around... and the initial eight became eighteen even though
we never saw some of the initial eight.' This being a course on education,
the disjunctions caused by this counter-cultural development itself became content from which professional and practical understanding could
be derived.

The most interesting and intransigent aspect – not an obstacle and only in some senses a problem – concerned the cultural disjunction between this course and students' experience of other ITT courses in their degree... Assessment also caused severe but richly 'learningful' problems, or at least grist for a mill, for much of the year. This was exacerbated by some unnecessary uncertainty as to what was actually required (partly information, partly problems of non-acculturation on both sides). In the end, the issue and processes of assessment afforded a rich vein for experiential learning and for reflecting on its role in teaching/learning situations generally. {230}

Theme Three: Active and interactive learning

Many teacher educators will squirm at the idea that learning could be anything but 'active and interactive'. Can there really be learning which does not involve activity of the mind or the engagement or interaction of the mind with something else, whether it be another person who is physically present, an artefact, a national environment or somebody's ideas presented in literary, graphic or artistic mode?

In the context of education for capability, however, active and interactive learning does attach particular importance to a sub-set of activity and interaction which is likely to help students apply learning to effective achievement in the social world, that is to say:

- to learning by making or doing;
- to learning from practice, particularly from practice in the environments in which students are preparing to work; and
- to interaction with other people, including in particular the kinds of interaction which will help individuals to communicate successfully with each other and to work collaboratively.

To value learning which has these dimensions is not to devalue critical reflection, reading and writing. And indeed one of the pedagogic challenges is to know how successfully to integrate these elements of learning with active and interactive learning more narrowly or prescriptively defined. However, part of what is being argued is that this more traditional scholarly engagement and reflection is insufficient for the development of capability within a variety of social fields including teaching.

Teacher education has of course been firmly based on active and experiential learning in schools and classrooms throughout the professional lives of today's teacher trainers, and beyond. The argument has never been as to whether this should be part of teacher training but rather more as to what extent, and about the relationship between the more theoretical/critical/reflective components and those which are more practical/active/experiential. A grounding in theory has from time to time been expected to provide the foundation for practice; practice has been expected to generate theory; and the two have been happily but not unproblematically resolved in the appealing notion of the reflective practitioner. Teacher education has perhaps more to offer than any other field of professional training in terms of the exploration of this relationship.

Similarly teacher educators have probably been at the forefront in higher education institutions in developing collaborative group work of a variety of kinds, not just in seminars, but also, for example, in the development of participatory group projects in the expressive arts or environmental studies. They have done the same in schools. For reasons of cost effectiveness, as well as educational value, more and more teacher education institutions are organizing teaching practice so that groups of four to twelve students are based in one school, with part of their experience involving working as a group.

This section presents some examples drawn from in-service and pre-service training chosen to illustrate different kinds of teaching and strategies being used to develop capability through active and interactive learning.

Enhancing the managerial effectiveness of teachers

At Manchester Polytechnic {120}, post-experience/postgraduate courses in education management at certificate, diploma and MSc levels incorporate a wide variety of active and interactive approaches, all of which promote learner responsibility and accountability in some way.

Certificate (two possible routes): Thirty teachers in 1990–91 became involved in the trial of one approach that involves assessment of prior learning, and the use of learning contracts in pursuing the Management Charter Initiative competency-based 'Management I' endorsement.

An alternative route is via six modules underpinned by the Kolb learning cycle and including a good deal of practice-related activity designed to assess competency and capability through reflection, self-evaluation and feedback by peers. The keeping of a 'management development portfolio' (journal) is an integral part of this learning process.

Diploma: This is centred around an 'applied problem-solving activity or a group consultancy project'. Small self-generated teams are linked with a client in an organization which has identified an issue requiring resolution. Teams investigate and complete a report to the client and are then assessed by a group viva on the process of their consultation.

MSc: This is an action learning year. Participants identify management action which they are undertaking in their organization and through action learning sets they proceed to examine their practice, culminating in a report to their client and a 'management learning review'.

Phase one of the diploma course provides a theoretical underpining through six modules arranged in three blocks that look at the following:

- the management of people;
- the management of resources; and
- the context for management.

Within this broad structure, there is scope for participants to address themes that are of immediate relevance to themselves as practitioners. The modular structure obviously allows the programme to be offered in separate units and facilitates the delivery of parts of the programme by other agencies.

The second phase is concerned with developing theory into practice – a process that will have begun in the first phase. This phase examines the dynamics of managing in a changing situation.

> Problems of application require the understanding of organizations as collections of diverse human beings and require from managers the ability to switch from being abstract conceptualizers to active interventionists. The management of change and intervention therefore provides the theme for the three modules that prepare course members for the applied problem-solving activity that follows. The phase begins with a weekend residential session designed to establish working teams and involving a range of activities focusing on generic management skills. {120}

The applied problem-solving activity places greater emphasis on learner responsibility and accountability, especially within teams.

> This requires course members, organized into small groups, to carry out a major consultancy exercise over several weeks in a school, college or other educational context. The outcomes of this will form the basis of the

assessment element of this phase. Course members produce and present a report on the activity for a named client in the situation. This group report, together with an individual learning review, the clients' comments and an oral presentation of the critical review of the experience to a panel of examiners forms the basis of the formal assessment. {120}

The other key developmental link for the first two phases is the 'management review portfolio'. This is intended to lend coherence and integration to the various components of the programme by encouraging participants to relate their learning to their own development and the world in which they live and work.

> This is a document kept by the course member recording his/her perception of the relationship between the daily experience of managing and the theoretical concerns and skill-based training of the course programme. Because of its confidential nature, the document is required but not assessed. It forms the basis of regular tutorial sessions in phases one and two. {120}

In the third and final phase, the course member engages on an individual 'management study' at a strategic level. To meet the validation requirements for an MSc, a masters dissertation is required. But in this case, responsibility and accountability are enhanced by 'the added dimension of the demands placed on the exercise by the fact that it must be presented to a manager who will have an informed view as to its worth'. This also represents a progression from the applied problem-solving activity of the second phase 'because responsibility for diagnosis and determination of appropriate recommendations for action now rest on the individual course member. The exercise requires intellectual skills of analysis and synthesis of the highest order, as well as command of the relevant literature and of the appropriate political and presentational skills.'

The notion of the critical practitioner community is taken one stage further at the MSc level.

> In regular sessions (at least three times a term), the course meets in seminar groups which discuss the progress of each individual study. These sessions explore critically the principles and processes of the studies and also offer advice and support. The process focuses not only on the particular issues of the study but also on the generalizable management learning illustrated by the case study each individual project provides as it unfolds. {120}

On most masters level courses the dissertation is a lone and often lonely journey, shared only with one's supervisor. Here, it provides a rigorous focal point for enhanced individual and group learning based on principles of responsibility and accountability.

PGCE collaborative enquiry

At the University of Sheffield {185}, the one-year PGCE (secondary) course calls for all students to work in small teams for five weeks in the summer term on a piece of collaborative work. This involves the collection and analysis of classroom-based or school-based data which will allow them to reflect on an issue which is of relevance to both the students and the schools involved. The end product is a report which is presented to the teachers involved and other students. The rest of the elements of the PGCE course are suspended while students work on their enquiry.

The collaborative enquiry seeks to relate principles of educating for capability in a variety of ways. The emphasis is on making students responsible for the management of their own learning, especially through providing opportunities for the conduct of enquiries on issues of relevance to the problems they confront within their own classrooms.

> The students are asked to identify their own problems for investigation; negotiate with the schools which they are going to work with; select appropriate seminars and consultations with specialists in the Division of Education in order to raise their knowledge of research methodology; plan their use of the five weeks allocated to the enquiry; provide regular feedback on progress; reconcile any difficulties within their own team; and consider how to share their work with other professionals and peers. {185}

The intention in this case is also to promote:

> ...a research-based model of teacher education which encourages a focus on the problematic nature of their 'art' and fosters an approach to personal and professional development which will underpin their future careers. {185}

The innovation grew naturally out of a course philosophy that centred on the value of the 'reflective practitioner'. The timing of the enquiry in the third term was intended:

> ...to harness the natural development of students' desire for autonomy and to build on their classroom practice after the completion of two 'block' teaching practice placements in different schools. Previous assignments

build towards this enquiry and so students are being encouraged to develop habits and attitudes supportive of research into their own practice. {185}

Comments drawn from evaluations by students and written and oral feedback from schools capture the flavour and value of the collaborative enquiry process within the context of the PGCE as a whole.

The students' comments also convey the extent to which such an experience was unfamiliar, in the context of their previous higher education.

- We found that collaborating on a given task proved interesting ... not only in what we discovered ... but also in what we learnt about ourselves. (student group)
- Although at the time 'vetting'... seemed to slow the progress of the group and even create a little acrimony, in retrospect it proved to be a worthwhile exercise. Firstly it maintained an atmosphere of healthy criticism. Secondly this encouraged individuals to look more critically at their own work. (student group) {185}

The comments from participating schools also indicate a changing perception of the department and what its students may have to offer to their further development.

- The report and its recommendations show a remarkable insight... The report is therefore of great value to the school and is at present being widely circulated.
- This exercise has also served to raise morale within the history department by highlighting the importance of our contribution to teacher training. (head of history) {185}

Theme Four: Assessment

Where in particular an assessment system is the gateway to a sought after qualification and an entitlement to practice, it exercises a powerful, perhaps overwhelming, influence over the programmes of study and the learning which it assesses. It carries its own messages to both students and tutors as to what really counts and what the institution or the course really values, never mind what is otherwise declared. So if capability principles are to be realized anywhere in teacher education, they have to be reflected in assessment systems.

What kind of features might we look for in such assessment practice? They might perhaps reflect the following principles:

- assessment procedures should give emphasis to what students are able to do in practice more than to what they know out of context;
- assessment procedures should encompass students' ability to reflect on and learn from experience, to put experience into perspective, to examine it critically, so that they are not limited to the here and now;
- assessment procedures should support and enhance students' self-knowledge, allowing them to make better informed judgements about their own capability and needs;
- assessment procedures should encourage and enable students to engage in self-assessment and to make that an integral part of their professional lives so that they can go on learning; and
- by extension, assessment procedures should include arrangements for students to collaborate in reciprocal and peer-group assessments so that they learn how to learn from each other.

Such principles have particular significance, of course, in the context of teacher education, because our students will have some responsibility for the assessment procedures which will in turn be employed in schools. They need therefore to think what is the best practice which they may take into schools as well as to be prepared to deal with the kind of assessment practices already well established in schools.

The examples chosen in this section are of the assessment strategies developed in two institutions.

Formative assessment through self-development diaries: developing the capable reflective practitioner

At the University of Wales {226}, first year undergraduates on a BA (Hons) Physical Education course are involved in a pilot scheme based on the use of self-development diaries. This sets out to make effective use of existing resources, in this case the college tutorial system. The intention is to carry forward this approach to years two and three in order to increase students' confidence and capability for taking responsibility for their own learning and development.

An initial 'counselling interview' helps students to clarify the personal, study and technical skills development required to satisfy course requirements. Following completion of the diary on a weekly basis for a term, the student returns for another session with the tutor, bringing with him/her for discussion a summary sheet of changes which have occurred. The diary remains the personal property of the student who may wish to keep it private.

Assessment at present is on an individual basis through discussions between tutor and tutee. It is hoped that the pilot scheme will indicate whether self-development diaries might serve as a useful means of developing self-awareness and assessment through the college tutorial system. If successful, their use will be carried through by students to years two and three.

This scheme was initiated as the result of staff involvement in an Enterprise in Higher Education seminar on Records of Achievement held at the University of Sheffield. Several approaches were presented. The tutors within the physical education department sought to make these various ideas their own in order to enhance support for students on the physical education course. The existing college tutorial system provided a framework within which to introduce this new dimension to the programme.

Self-development diaries are seen in this context as 'tools to enable students to identify personal strengths and weaknesses and to record progress or regression in these areas'. In capability terms, the diaries seek to promote:

- heightened self-awareness;
- developing ability to self-evaluate strengths and weaknesses;
- an increasing awareness of the various sources of information available to, and used by, the individual for assessment;
- recognition of the importance of interactive personal skills in achieving progress;
- an increased awareness for the need to set goals in both the short and the long term, and to identify ways of achieving those goals;
- the ability of students to evaluate for themselves, progress and regression in relation to their starting points and their learning aims and objectives, with an increased awareness of the various sources of information individuals can use for self-assessment; and
- the capability of students in finding ways of achieving identified goals and acting on the outcomes of self and peer review of progress. {226}

The use of self-development diaries is not intended as a bolt-on innovation but, rather, as a means of completing and supporting course requirements in various ways. Emphasis in particular is placed on:

- the effective use of time, and learning how to manage leisure and professional priorities;
- the use of staff and peer support in identifying and acknowledging strengths and weaknesses – by declaring these, declaring intentions for change and recording change in writing, students become more

confident about identifying and achieving appropriate personal and professional development goals; and
- the ongoing responsibility of students for their own professional development. Through the diaries, students are able to set personal attainment goals which are of particular importance to themselves and, with counselling, to plan strategies for achieving these targets. Successes and problems are recognized through counselling. {226}

In this case, continual self-assessment supported by the self-development diary is the key vehicle for driving the development of capability.

For any learner to become more capable, there must be an assessment, preferably by the self, of the progress which is being made. The self-development diaries support and complement the Physical Education course objective to produce students who can monitor and evaluate their own development. {226}

Recording progress and achievement
At Westminster College {231}, the 'record of progress and achievement' (RPA) on the PGCE course (with approximately 150 students, secondary and primary) involves the profiling of skills and competency in teacher education. It involves the development of negotiated profiles, individual action plans, and self- and peer-assessment. The RPA documentation identifies key stages within the course for needs analysis, identification of achievement and target-setting. The courses are assessed by school-focused assignments and school experience of which the criteria relate to capability.

The scheme was introduced in September 1989 and piloted during the 1989/1990 academic year. A revised version was in operation in 1990/1991 and further developments were incorporated for the third year.

The RPA was introduced as a means of contributing to the overall quality of student learning and the development of professional competence and capability through explicit attention to the following.

- *Analysis of learning needs* starting with assessment of prior learning, linked to the establishment of action plans, evaluation of experience, review and reformulation in the light of experience;
- *Planning and organization of own learning* in college and schools, using specific activities to focus development, such as technology

skills, practical experience, in-depth investigation of cross-curricular themes (eg, equal opportunities, industrial awareness);

- *Negotiating learning goals* constantly in respect of college and school experience, with teachers, tutors and individually with peers;
- *Clarifying the nature of their accountability for specific learning outcomes* through review of experience, identifying achievement and priorities for development linked to self- and negotiated evaluation;
- *Evidence of achievement* against intended outcomes follows from target-setting linked to stages of review and re-assessment;
- *Assessing of learning outcomes* through target-setting and review and opportunities to take responsibility for pupil learning in schools;
- *Development of capability and responsibility* through focusing on individual responsibility linked to opportunities for peer review. While the views of tutors and teachers are important, the emphasis throughout is on weaning students away from satisfying others to establishing self-confidence in individual judgement;
- *Transferability and adaptability* are enhanced through the emphasis on self-evaluation, together with the range of school experience which is offered. Of particular note here is the opportunity for inner-city, multicultural experience which offers opportunities to identify new targets and to adapt achievements to new circumstances;
- *Learning to take responsibility and be accountable* is a natural consequence of the framework and the emphasis on self-evaluation and review which building the RPA into the course process promotes;
- *Confidence in individual self-worth and the ability to act decisively* are enhanced through self- and peer-review, the variety of experiences and the responsibility, in discussion with others, for identifying individual progress targets;
- *Active learning* is central in a course aimed at preparing new teachers and the RPA helps graduate students adjust to new patterns of learning, not only for themselves but through reflection on their own experience, to have the confidence to build this into the learning experiences of their pupils. {231}

As resources become increasingly constrained, the use of existing time for new developments becomes increasingly important: 'A range of meetings has been arranged, many of which were not additional to what would otherwise have been needed (eg, school experience support meetings, evaluation meetings with teachers, team meetings).' But finding time was always a problem: 'The pressures from other work meant that tutors and teachers were too swamped with other things to give student profiles full attention. The main obstacle lay in finding adequate time to involve tutors in the innovation in such a way that they all felt that they had ownership of it. It appeared to be the development of the few, which was then imposed on others, which caused some active and passive opposition. To overcome this, as wide a group of tutors as possible were involved in further developments.'

The introduction of such a scheme also raises wider issues in the context of other developments in the professional lives of teachers:

> The development has raised the question of how the RPA links in philosophically, educationally and logistically into the school appraisal system, and in particular into the guidance programme offered to probationers in the first year of teaching. {231}

The benefits to students identified through internal evaluation (questionnaires and meetings) are seen as considerable:

> ...more structured guidance, better quality of discussion between student, tutor and teachers, greater evidence of students identifying their own agendas for future development, students having more confidence in school situations, more self-sufficiency, and a greater tendency to seek advice at the right time. {231}

The introduction of this approach also creates a coherence of experience across the school and HE learning contexts.

> It allows students greater understanding of records of achievement systems being used in schools, since they are operating pupil records and profiles in schools at the same time as they are using the RPA at their own level. {231}

Conclusion

We have encountered a number of difficulties in selecting and presenting examples for this chapter. The first arose from the fact that the developments we are describing are very much interconnected. Several of the examples could, of course, with just a little adjustment, have fitted into more than one theme.

The second difficulty was the need to balance the demands of brevity with the need to provide enough detail and context to make sense of an initiative. We have probably erred on the side of brevity, and we urge readers to approach institutions directly for more information.

The third difficulty was in leaving out a large number of accounts of fertile and intriguing innovation which we would like to have included. The material submitted (itself only a fraction of what we could have sought) represents something of a tribute to the rarely acknowledged capacity for innovation and creativity of teacher educators in an environment so heavy with ignorant criticism that they could have been excused for giving up in despair.

The examples show, however, that teacher educators are committed to capability in their students – even if they do not commonly use the language of capability – and are well advanced, as one would hope specialists in education would be, in innovative approaches to capability.

The reported experience thus far raises a number of critical issues for teacher educators. Among these are:

- How can the principles of capability here illustrated best be protected and fostered in a context of increasing centralized regulation of the content and methodology of teacher education?
- In particular, how can we resist the tendency to pack the initial teacher education curriculum (especially the PGCE) with acres of pre-specified content?
- What is the relationship of the rhetoric of *capability* with that of *enterprise* and with that of the *reflective practitioner*? Do we have three ideologies here? Or two? Or can they be reconciled in one?
- What model of competency should emerge as the dominant one in the next year or two? What model do we see as supportive of capability principles – broad generic competences in which intelligence and sensitivity in context feature prominently? Which model is likely to undermine such capability – long lists of atomized performances?
- As higher education institutions are measured increasingly against 'quality' criteria, how can we ensure that those criteria enshrine rather than exclude the principles and practice conducive to capability in pre-service and in-service teachers?

References
Handy, C. (1989) *The Age of Unreason* London: Business Books.
Peters, T. (1987) *Thriving on Chaos*. London: Macmillan.

Part Three: The Challenges

Chapter Nine
Educating for Capability:
Some Obstacles and Ways Forward

John Stephenson and Susan Weil

Higher Education for Capability presents major challenges for students, teachers, course designers, validators, institutional managers, employers and external funding agencies. This final chapter focuses on the issues arising from the experiences of those who are introducing learner responsibility and accountability in the context of those challenges and suggests possible ways forward.

The challenge for students
The suppliers of examples report considerable and varied benefits for students who successfully manage their own learning. A compilation of typical claims shows:

> ...improved study skills, higher motivation, a greater understanding of theory than when traditional methods were used, more reading done, a high quality of presentations , greater student confidence with regard to taking responsibility for their learning and working at their own pace within their chosen environment; more confidence and capability in negotiating and working in teams; and revitalized tutor morale and communication.

Some suppliers also report initial scepticism and resistance among a small minority of students – even within groups where the benefits have been great. Initial student resistance can also be a deterrent to cautious teachers and institutions. It is important that staff and students understand the bases of student resistance if they are to take steps to maximize student benefit. There appear to be six main causes of resistance:

(1) student expectations of teacher roles, based on prior and parallel experience;
(2) fear of failure being attributed to their own inadequacies;
(3) the absence of traditional measures of progress, such as the volume of lecture notes and comparing assignment grades with fellow students;
(4) concern that work initiated by themselves may not be taken seriously by outsiders;
(5) short-term aspirations focused on the achievement of qualifications by the least effort; and
(6) lack of experience and confidence with this approach to learning.

These factors have most significance in mixed-mode environments, where 'cultural disjunction' exacerbates the students' concerns about being treated differently, being left behind or, worse, 'being experimented on'.

The examples illustrate a number of ways in which student resistance can be addressed. They include:

- providing students with a clear rationale for the new approach, together with the time to discuss its relevance and meaning;
- helping students to review the relevance of the new approach to their previous experience and longer term aspirations;
- early exposure of students to potential professional environments and practitioners, with a focus on the knowledge, skills and qualities needed for good performance;
- the provision of peer support, with time explicitly devoted to the exploration of process problems
- an unequivocal commitment to students learning from the experiences of responsibility and accountability, with an emphasis on critical dialogue between student and tutor about the student's progress, and the development of skills of self-monitoring;
- helping students to review the progress they are making in their specialist studies;
- confirmation of the value of the process from established external bodies; and
- staged introduction to responsibility and accountability.

Experience shows that these measures promote a sense of student ownership and control over their own learning, give reassurance about its value, establish the intellectual as well as functional credibility of the process, help students to address for themselves the basis of any scepticism they may have and provide an expanding dossier of evidence of student progress.

The challenge for teachers

The wider introduction of capability approaches is to a large extent dependent on successful initiatives by subject teachers. The art and design experience reported in Chapter Three shows it is possible for a wide variety of teachers, many of them part-time, to manage whole programmes of study in which students are helped to be responsible and accountable for their own learning. The capability approach is traditional in art and design; teachers are imbued with its values and a belief in its relevance; it is part of their own educational experience and current professional practice. To educate for capability in art and design is to conform with the culture. Teachers in many other disciplines – to varying degrees – have additional and more difficult tasks. They have to devise approaches which are new to their culture and have the confidence and skill to implement them. They have to cope with cultural disjunction, not only with some of their colleagues but also with their own substantial but different experience. They have to address the issues of their own identity and role.

The examples in Part Two present a useful source of information on the nature of the difficulties which teachers have to address, and ways in which they might be overcome. The difficulties are only partly related to the mastery of unfamiliar techniques; the major difficulties relate to the teachers' perceptions of their roles. Some staff have inhibitions about the very concept of passing responsibility to students. There is a fear of letting go; that students may not learn what the teacher wants them to learn; that, once the traditional function of transmitting information has gone, the residual roles will be trivial; that teachers may not always be able to answer students' questions; and that a process consultant has less status than a subject expert, and less opportunity for promotion in a system that favours subject expertise and research. There are inhibitions related to teacher perceptions of student readiness: students cannot be trusted to get on with things; they have had no experience of taking responsibility; the standard of their work will suffer; they will make unreasonable demands on the teacher's time; it is not possible to manage so many different student interests at the same time; and that they will be disadvantaged in terms of professional recognition.

Such concerns are bound up with genuine concern for the students' progress and future opportunities. In the eyes of the traditional teacher, because student progress is seen to be directly related to the quality of teacher transmitted expertise, it would be irresponsible for the teacher to let go. The power of this feeling of teacher responsibility should not be underestimated. Its influence continues long after staff have bitten the bullet and have seen at first hand that learner responsibility and accountability are both feasible and educationally productive. Our correspondents report feelings of guilt about their new roles, that somehow they are abdicating their 'real' duties. To counter this, some teachers retain the practices of 'wealthier times' by trying to be available for all possible student needs and requests, in addition to taking on the demanding and complex tasks of the new order. Others go in the opposite direction and leave students to their own devices, fearful that any intervention or instruction by them would weaken the delicate flower of student-managed learning. Uncertainty about which way to go contributes to feelings of being exposed, insecure and at risk.

Our correspondents also report that the change from content provider to 'learning assistant' can be rewarding and intellectually challenging. To engage students in critical dialogue about fundamental concepts, to be open about their own struggles with particular content areas, to share the pain and excitement of what it means to be a scholar, to help students to find their way through the growing mass of references and information sources, to test assumptions against practice, to help students 'talk it through', and to explore the provisional nature of what we currently accept as knowledge are more challenging and intellectually satisfying activities than the sterile communication of 'certain' knowledge and information. A capability approach, far from de-skilling specialist academics, can give new status to their scholarship; for good measure it prepares students for learning through the rest of their lives. Contributors report feeling revitalized by the freshness of their interactions with students which in turn revitalizes departments where morale is low.

Higher Education for Capability encourages student negotiated learning, not student self-determination (Chapter Two). Negotiation is a two-way process, with tutors as active participants, not as passive gatekeepers. Negotiation makes it possible for tutors to participate in the students' learning, pressing for clarity of purpose, challenging assumptions, encouraging the development and testing of propositions and supporting students in critical reviews of the development of their personal skills and understanding. The tutor can raise students' awareness of different theoretical perspectives and give access to supporting specialist resources and sources.

Critical dialogue is relevant at all stages – when students are planning their programmes, carrying them out and grappling with the criteria and mode of assessment.

A number of strategies have helped tutors to cross the barrier from scepticism and wariness to intellectual challenge and enthusiasm.

Small initial steps, for instance, have helped a number of correspondents to 'get their feet wet', building confidence incrementally. A useful and relatively safe first step is for subject-based staff to articulate the skills which they hope their students derive from their courses and to consider the kinds of learning experiences most likely to develop them. Some staff were stimulated to introduce changes in response to follow-up studies of graduate appraisals of the skills they wished they had developed on their undergraduate courses. Giving students responsibility for their own projects is the most frequently mentioned initiative; the most useful further step is to focus the students' attention on the learning processes and learning outcomes of the project. Another effective first step, (effective because it ensures student interest and gets to the heart of the capability process) is for tutors to initiate discussion with students about the criteria used in their final assessment. Those who have tried this report higher student motivation, improved student performance and student debate about the meaning and relevance of the course aims and objectives.

Greater self-discipline has also been of assistance. The capability teacher has a complex set of duties which need to be well managed if the tutor is to flourish. Many tasks are of an administrative nature. There are many students with different problems, many records to keep, placements to arrange and supervise, student reports to read, meetings to attend, contracts to review and scholarship to sustain. With innovations there are strategies to devise, people to persuade, plans to prepare, approvals to be sought and students to recruit. Without good time management, urgent administration can exclude time out for reflection. Students need to be briefed of the constraints and helped to work within them. Well-disciplined tutors also present good models for students, particularly if the students themselves need reassurance; over-pressed and disorganized teachers convey uncertainty and doubt.

Effective team-working can spread burdens and provide a forum for peer-related critical dialogue. As with students, a support group can help tutors address issues of concern. Staff logs or diaries and co-counselling can help tutors build up their own confidence in the process as well as providing experience with techniques useful for students.

Staff development based on capability principles can provide tutors with first-hand experience of the processes they might use with their students. The most effective staff development programmes reported to us involve staff working together, with guidance, assessing their own development needs, setting targets, monitoring their progress and recording their learning while introducing capability approaches into their own teaching programmes. As with students, so with staff: the medium is the message. The introduction of capability into a formal programme of staff development provides support, time and occasion for staff reflection about the issues and the learning they are deriving from the experience of introducing capability approaches.

The Enterprise in Higher Education Initiative has been particularly successful in bringing about change because it has paid for time and practical support for staff to talk through the issues, to prepare plans, to seek advice and to reflect on their progress.

Affiliation with fellow specialists is an important staff need. Persuasion from education experts is less potent than the encouragement and example of respected figures within the same field. Belief in the distinctive needs of teaching particular subjects is strong; reassurance from people dealing with the same specialist issues is welcomed. Informal networks and databases which cross institutional boundaries are increasingly being developed for the exchange of ideas and the sharing of concerns.

Contact with employers can help tutors appreciate the relevance of their courses to the world of work. A number of academics in non-vocational areas have found it useful to demonstrate the vocational relevance of the skills and qualities their students develop. Employers can provide encouragement, study opportunities and resources for capability-orientated activities.

Overall, the experience of the examples submitted is that most of the educational and practical obstacles facing staff can be overcome. The most challenging difficulties teachers have to overcome relate to academic values and self-esteem. Both of these legitimate concerns can be addressed by focusing attention on the quality of student and staff learning engendered by greater student responsibility and accountability. One interesting assertion is that once staff have progressed to working effectively with learner responsibility and accountability they do not wish to return to their former practices.

The challenge for course designers

Higher Education for Capability invites a new approach to course design. Capability programmes consist of frameworks within which student negotiation can take place. If the content and mode of assessment of part or the whole of a course are negotiated by the student, it is no longer possible to describe courses in terms of the content to be covered. Instead, course design needs to focus on the processes involved, the systems of tutorial and resource support, the procedures to be followed, the general objectives to be reached, the criteria which have to be met and the rigour with which they will be judged.

The examples illustrate that although much can be achieved by teachers within the confines of their own discrete areas of responsibility, the student experience is often small scale, inevitably affecting only a proportion of the student's total higher education. Some of the key elements necessary to provide a coherent capability experience, such as admissions policy, student progression, timetables, quality assurance procedures, validation, resource availability and assessments for final qualifications, are beyond the control of individual teachers. Many teachers report having to work against course structures; much more could be achieved if the course structures themselves were designed to develop student capability.

Educating for capability involves a re-ordering of the relationship between teacher and student, and between content and process. Course structures should provide the right balance and relationship between three activities: giving students access to content; helping students prepare for and exercise responsibility for their own programmes of study; and promoting reflection on the learning which takes place. Many conventional courses are designed only around the first of these, the delivery of teacher-determined content with some space for reflection on the material delivered. A capability approach puts the emphasis on the planning and reviewing of student learning by the students themselves, supported by activities (lectures, using the library, workshops, assignments, projects, consultancies, placements, etc) which enable the students to engage and understand content relevant to their explicit needs and aspirations. Far from diminishing the status of content, the experience reported in the examples indicates that students in this second model can cover a considerable amount of content and reach deeper levels of understanding.

If students are to manage their own learning, content needs will vary and this will involve access to more varied, flexible and readily available sources than reliance on a predetermined lecture programme. The experience also suggests that, where whole programmes of study are concerned, students benefit from being in process groups which provide opportunities for peer support and student/tutor dialogue.

If time is to be found for process activities, the timetable cannot be filled with formal lectures or workshop demonstrations. Pressure on staff resources and the lower cost of desk-top publishing are encouraging many courses to make lecture notes available on disk or in packages stored in the library. New data storage and retrieval systems mean that students access this teacher-produced material in the context of other sources of information. Library-based lecture material makes it easier for students to cross boundaries into other specialist areas. The examples also show that active and interactive learning can expose students to a greater variety of information sources and expertise, as well as involving students in the application of knowledge and skills.

One problem highlighted in the examples is the danger that students can be left too much to their own devices, that staff will think that activities and resource availability will suffice. Placements, for instance, give students experience of being in environments relevant to their studies, but without time and energy devoted to the support of student planning and reflection there may be little learning from the experience. Package-based lecture material without time for planning and reflection on its relevance can just as easily lead to teacher-dependent content acquisition and regurgitation.

Assuring credibility through student accountability
The credibility of student-managed learning with employers, accrediting bodies, teachers and the students themselves is enhanced when the course structure places obligations on students to justify their intentions and account for their learning, and when the timetable makes time and support available for students to do so. Moreover, student accountability conducted with rigour is a major vehicle for the development of student confidence in higher level capabilities related to evaluating their own performance, explaining what they are about and learning from their own experiences. It represents a conscious commitment to reflection on learning, to the building up of accumulated knowledge and skill and developing the means of doing so, and to the integration of student learning from their activities in 'the field'.

The capability of students, the quality of their learning and the credibility of their programmes are enhanced when course structures require students to reflect on and give account of:

- their prior learning and future intentions (at admissions and the start of courses);
- the relevance of their proposed programmes of study (at admissions and in the context of negotiation);
- their intended learning outcomes, how they will be achieved and how they will be demonstrated (at approvals of plans for programmes and assessment);
- the intended and unexpected learning they are deriving from active and interactive learning (at stage or monitoring assessments); and
- the nature, relevance and value of their achievements (at formal assessments).

Learning contracts are increasingly being used as devices for structuring student initiative within a framework of accountability. Where contracts cover all of the above stages of a student's experience, there is an opportunity for students to prepare coherent and integrated programmes of study. Where contracts are renegotiable they can respond to unplanned learning. Contracts make it possible for courses to establish formal approval or registration procedures which in turn give reassurance to students and outsiders.

A major issue mentioned by some of our correspondents concerns the criteria used for the approval of student learning contracts. In some cases the criteria are externally determined and relate to specific areas of content thereby reducing scope for student initiative; in others they are not clearly articulated, leaving students vulnerable to unexplained judgements and a pernicious form of control. The approval of learning contracts requires open and clear criteria related to the level and scope of the awards students are seeking, leaving students to propose specific activities and areas of study. Some of our correspondents have found the preparation of those criteria to be a valuable staff development activity in its own right.

The examples submitted give insights into a number of more specific course design issues, namely, admissions, progression, modular structures and assessment.

Admissions

It greatly helps capability teachers when admission to capability-orientated courses is based in part on students' potential for taking responsibility for their own learning. Though significant changes are under way (see below), entry based on A level scores still predominates in many areas. The difficulty with A level courses is that they use traditional teaching methods and encourage students to rely heavily on their teachers. Many academics have told us that they cannot introduce capability programmes because students recruited straight from school are not able, or do not wish, to take responsibility for even part of their own educational development. This assumption is used to justify the continuation of didactic approaches to teaching in undergraduate education. Staff, in other words, collude with the perpetuation of alleged student inability to manage their own development rather than introduce students to approaches more appropriate to higher centres of learning and the development of capability.

This collusion over teacher-dependent styles of education invites the following satire, a self-justifying cycle.

> We take high A level score people; they are not used to being given responsibility for their learning so we do not give them any; our students do well when spoon-fed and they pass our exams based on the regurgitation of spoon-fed material; employers recruit our students because of our A level points policy and complain about the lack of capability in graduates; we get high quality ratings because our students have high A level points and get first destination jobs; we are able to attract even more applicants because of our high public rating and first destination reputation so we can push up the A level average score at entry still further and defend A levels as the gold-standard of quality in HE.

The apparent ease with which blue-chip courses can fill their places encourages complacency about the relevance of traditional admissions procedures. Changing the regulations, criteria and procedures for the admission of students to courses to include applicants' appraisals of their own prior experience is an effective way of encouraging the development of capability on the course itself. A number of the examples had their origin in teachers having to take account of individual student needs and differences within the broader groups they were receiving. Growing confidence in the techniques of accrediting prior experience and learning (APEL), and the newly launched National Record of Achievements are making it more feasible for admissions tutors to look for evidence of capability potential. Changes in the school curriculum associated with GCSE and TVEI are giving more of the conventional intake experience of programme negotiation and skills development.

Structural progression

Some courses put students in at the deep end; most prefer to help students move gradually to higher levels of responsibility. A number of examples achieve progress to student responsibility by providing a good grounding in key skills and concepts in the early stages and allowing student negotiation based on that foundation for the later stages; some have progressively more permissive objectives for each stage of a course; others provide students with early exposure to the practical or professional context in which they wish to work to give them sufficient experience of the knowledge and skills requirements on which to base their proposals. The favoured gradual approach is successful if, from the outset, students and staff are aware of the overall strategy; knowledge of what is to come can encourage students to explore the relevance of earlier work to their future interests.

Modularization

The rationale for the widespread modularization of courses includes more effective resource management and greater student mobility; it does not necessarily imply any real change in the nature and quality of the learning experiences of students within those modules. Choosing from a fixed menu is a limited form of giving students responsibility for learning. There is concern amongst some correspondents that the modular solution makes it much more difficult for students to manage their overall personal and academic progression in response to their growing understanding of their needs; some complain that 'pick and mix' approaches to student planning avoid any obligation to address the issue of course coherence; others remark that relatively short self-contained units encourage a content-dominated curriculum. The accumulation of credits can take precedence over the students taking responsibility for their learning and development.

On the other hand, the development of modular schemes has given many of our correspondents the opportunity to develop capability programmes. Course teams have begun to make unit objectives more explicit which in turn has encouraged discussion of personal skills and qualities, and the ways of developing them. Progression towards capability can be helped if, say, all level two modules have objectives which allow greater student responsibility than do level one objectives. Others have found it possible to introduce radical change within the confines of one module without challenging the educational basis of the whole of their department. Others have found that cross-movement of students makes it impossible to make assumptions about common expertise of module entrants and have found it useful to introduce learning contracts leading to general criteria for success at the end. One interesting solution to the problem of course coherence is to ask students to incorporate their choice of modules within an overall learning contract in which the mix is justified in terms of the students' expertise and long-term intentions. It is also possible for courses to establish modules explicitly devoted to student/tutor dialogue on the planning of the rest of the programme, the monitoring and review of progress, and critical reviews on student learning and outcomes. The learning from these activities can thereby be recognized and contribute to the student's overall assessment.

Assessments

Most of the examples of capability assessments do not contribute towards the students' degrees; the traditional three-hour unseen written examination still prevails across much of the higher education system. There is, nevertheless, a growing expertise in the use of assessment which: (1) focuses on the application of knowledge and skills; (2) involves students in their own assessments; (3) accommodates the assessment of students in groups, and (4) involves professional practitioners and potential employers. Alternatives to the three-hour unseen paper include:

- student negotiated projects or dissertations on issues or problems associated with an external context, such as the work-place or community activity;
- consultancy contracts negotiated with outside clients replicating work-place conditions and using professional criteria of success;
- collaborative projects in which individually negotiated contracts within the group make it possible to distinguish individual contributions and performance;
- critical reviews of the students' programme, learning and achievements, prepared by the students themselves, with supporting evidence from peers, employers, academics and their own teachers; and
- profiles of student development and records of student achievement produced by the students themselves as part of their monitoring assessment.

Each of the above gives students a high degree of personal responsibility, is an effective learning activity in its own right, and provides a great deal of information about what students can do and have done. Each enables students to demonstrate their personal skills and qualities through the assessment of their specialist knowledge and skills.

The successful integration of personal skills and specialist knowledge in the same assessment is particularly interesting in the context of current debates about learning outcomes and competences. The separate assessment of precisely defined skills in isolation from their integration with other qualities disembodies human capability and fails to indicate the students' ability to use skills in combination with other skills and specialist knowledge in the context of problems or issues relevant to the students' longer term personal and vocational development. Moreover, student negotiated assessments allow for a wider definition of skills and qualities than those contained within most course programmes, and invites greater understanding of their nature and relevance.

There is considerable interest in self- and peer-assessment, partly because judging one's own performance is an important part of capability, but also because it is a way of stimulating and systematizing reflection on progress and the learning process. Many have reported student reluctance to give fail marks to peers or to give high marks to themselves, even when they feel they might be justified. These understandable inhibitions can be overcome if students are assessed not on the marks they award but on their ability to present a critical evaluation. The more we use self-assessments, peer-assessments, work completed off campus and work in response to programmes negotiated by students, the more we need to address the issue of accountability. Publication of the criteria used in judging student performance in formal assessments, the involvement of relevant external figures such as professional practitioners, and the use of external examiners sympathetic to the aims of capability education, have established the credibility of student involvement in their own final assessment in the art and design field, and would do so in other areas.

The challenge for accrediting bodies

Once designed, higher education programmes need to be approved. Polytechnic courses have been validated by the Council for National Academic Awards (CNAA), university courses by their Senates and courses from both sectors are accredited by professional bodies. External validation is important for capability courses. Students need reassurance that their programmes will lead to recognized qualifications; the wider world needs assurance that the quality of student negotiated activities is satisfactory. The method of validation is a crucial factor as the contrasting experiences of the professional bodies and the CNAA illustrate.

Professional bodies, of course, vary and the observations which follow represent the general not the total picture. The involvement of professional bodies in the accreditation of higher education programmes ought not to be an obstacle to the introduction of education for capability. Professionals need specialist skills and knowledge; they also need to be aware of their limitations, capable of learning new skills and acquiring new information, effective in collaboration with other professionals from their own and from other fields, and able to relate well to clients. They need to be capable. Yet a frequently expressed reason voiced by academics for not introducing capability approaches is that 'the professional body would not allow it'. Staff responsible for some of the examples in Part Two have deliberately opted not to seek professional recognition because, they claim, the capability features of their programmes would have to be removed. Our information is that progress towards the introduction of capability into programmes leading to professional recognition is proceeding slowly and patchily.

It is interesting to note the experience of art and design. British designers are highly regarded world-wide. A high proportion of design graduates work as designers. They are sought after by overseas companies. There is no tradition of regulation by professional bodies and a high number of the tutors work in professional practice themselves. The students have to earn their employment by their professional competence, not by the academic credits they gain on accredited taught courses. On the other hand, in business, finance and law, employers have reported dissatisfaction with professionally prepared graduates and prefer to train their own staff recruited from 'non-relevant' disciplines.

Here are some of the obstacles perceived by academics.

•   Members of review panels are often unaware of the educational advantages of involving students in the design, operation and assessment of their own programmes of study.
•   There is a lack of flexibility in the range of approved assessment techniques; unseen written examinations predominate.
•   Accreditation is often based on the structure, content and staff/student contact hours of courses rather than on the demonstration of professional capability.

It is difficult to judge the extent to which these concerns are excuses for lack of action or genuine obstacles to change. Sometimes the conservatism resides within academic boards and senates.

On their part, the professional bodies have an obligation to protect the interests of clients and customers by ensuring that members have appropriate standards of competence. They have traditionally seen accreditation of courses on the basis of their content as the main means of securing that assurance. This pressure is increasing in Europe. Many bodies also argue that their procedures are more flexible than some academics assume, that recent changes in their regulations are more forward-looking and that progress would be made if more innovative proposals were submitted.

Our discussions with both sides have suggested a number of ways forward.

- Further dialogue on the most appropriate balance between knowledge and skills.
- A formal system of post-initial and continuing professional education and development on which continuing membership is dependent, thereby freeing initial higher education programmes to concentrate on helping students to develop mastery of essential concepts, gain experience of the nature and values of the profession and build confidence in their ability to continue to learn from their experiences.
- The inclusion on review panels of more leading-edge practitioners and employers, people with an understanding of capability processes and a commitment to the development of effective professional performance, and fewer people who are there by virtue of seniority and past achievement.
- The use of criteria for accreditation couched more in terms of capability outcomes and appropriate learning experiences, and less in terms of prescribed content.
- Illustrative syllabuses based on capability principles.
- Procedures for the accreditation of learning contracts negotiated between students, professionally relevant employers and higher education institutions, probably through delegated responsibility.

- Encouragement for the use of assessments based on how students use their professional knowledge rather than their mere possession of that knowledge.
- Jointly prepared initiatives – between academics and professional bodies – based on capability principles.

- More use of student negotiated 'live projects' with local employers or client-based professional practices jointly supervised by college staff and professional practitioners.

In contrast, there are many examples of educating for capability on courses that previously received validation by the Council for National Academic Awards (CNAA) or in institutions with CNAA delegated powers of validation. The CNAA approach to external validation has been based on four principles, all of them consistent with the code of practice advocated by Higher Education for Capability for the accreditation of courses devised by students.

(1) Responsibility for the preparation of detailed proposals about content, process and methods of assessment rests with the institutions.
(2) General criteria and procedures related to the level of courses and the development of personal qualities relevant to capability are published by the CNAA.
(3) Proposals for courses have to be justified in terms of the published general criteria of the CNAA.
(4) The review panels include people drawn from other institutions, employers and relevant professional bodies.

The personal qualities referred to in item (2) above are:

...the development of students' intellectual and imaginative powers; their understanding and judgement; their problem-solving skills; their ability to communicate; their ability to see relationships within what they have learnt and to perceive their field of study in a broader perspective... the development of an enquiring, analytical and creative approach, encouraging independent judgement and critical self-awareness. (*CNNA Handbook, 1989*)

In other words, the criteria against which accountability is to be judged have been made explicit.

The success of this approach can be judged by the fact that polytechnics have raised their reputation for the quality of their work to the point where self-validation is no longer seen as a contentious issue. With the demise of the CNAA and the designation of polytechnics as self-validating institutions, it is important that the four principles continue to be applied by academic boards and are transferred to senates as the universities build up their quality assurance procedures in readiness for the new funding arrangements.

The differences between the influences of the CNAA and the professional bodies on the design of capability courses may well be related to the fact that the former responds to local initiative and is concerned with learning outcomes and the development of skills, and the latter constrain local initiative by predetermining the content.

The challenge for higher education institutions

The nature and style of management and leadership in higher education institutions (HEIs) have a significant influence in the development of capability. As our examples indicate, most initiatives have come from individual or groups of academics working within institutional structures which were developed to support a very different tradition of education. New approaches inevitably test these structures. Navigating the pathways to change can be unnecessarily burdensome, requiring high commitment and political ingenuity for success. If the more obvious points of tension are removed, more initiatives can be made and the bluff of the constrained innovators who complain that 'the system is against them' can be called. With staff morale being tested by frequent and major changes in funding and administrative arrangements, help and positive encouragement for educational development would pay dividends.

Areas where action by HEIs would be most effective are institutional ethos, staffing policies, physical resources, educational resources, and quality assurance procedures.

Institutional ethos: the learning institution

In capability-orientated institutions, learning is a common experience shared, at different levels and in different contexts, by researchers, teachers and students. Capability students can very well learn from and alongside researchers. Undergraduate experience of learner responsibility and accountability would greatly diminish the need to prepare postgraduate students for carrying out their own work, thereby reducing lead-times and doctorate wastage rates. Specialist teachers who are also scholars can help and enthuse students with their own learning, discussing concepts, current issues, underlying principles and methods of study. Teachers, in turn, can learn from the activities of their students.

A commitment to being 'a learning institution' fits well with a commitment to total quality management. TQM involves all participants (in a learning institution this would also include students) in taking more responsibility for raising the quality of their activities and working environment in accordance with the stated aims of the institution. The development of Higher Education for Capability could flourish in such institutions. Those responsible for the learning, administrative and physical environments would be sensitive to the needs of students taking responsibility for their own learning; they would see the changing of procedures to accommodate new needs as progress, not a burden. Rigid distinctions between those institutions mainly concerned with 'research' and those mainly concerned with 'teaching' may distract attention from their common interest in learning, encouraging the latter to see students as people who are there to be taught rather than to learn how to be capable learners.

With a commitment to being responsive to the learning needs of students, institutions can be effective in both attracting and retaining groups not previously attracted or able to apply. The examples in Part Two illustrate the many ways in which a capability approach has been found to be appropriate for varied intakes of students; indeed, in some cases capability programmes were devised precisely to cope with the variety of students coming forward. Widening access is not just a matter of squeezing more in. It also means helping those attracted to build on their distinctive experiences and work towards their intended personal or vocational goals.

Staffing issues

Many of our correspondents refer to low staff morale and a lack of support from within their institutions. Many would welcome a more pro-active stance by middle and upper management to replace their normal experience of constantly having to push for support. Promotion policies, appraisals, resource support and recognition are among the issues raised.

The tying of academic staff promotions to research and publications can discourage ambitious staff from participating in the development of innovation in teaching. If staff spend time on curriculum development, they have less time to devote to preparing publications, unless they work twice as hard and do both. Investment of personal time, intellectual rigour and emotional commitment can be just as great for the successful introduction of innovations in teaching as for the preparation of academic publications for one's CV. If the innovations relate to the development of programmes based on capability principles, the pay-off for the department in terms of quality of student learning and relevance to the outside world can be considerable.

Reservations expressed about staff appraisal systems focus on two issues. First, there is concern that appraisal does not always use criteria related to the institution's mission statement or goals, particularly where goals refer to the development of student capability, relevance to the wider community and responsiveness to the educational and employment needs of students.

The second concern about staff appraisal relates to the use of student feedback on staff performance, particularly where capability programmes are being developed within a predominantly traditional teaching environment. Student feedback on standard questionnaires is likely to focus on styles of delivery, the adequacy of notes and other features of didactic teaching. Research on student responses to being given responsibility for the first time refers to periods of stress and disorientation as students struggle with the demands of taking responsibility, perhaps causing temporary frustration with the course and their tutors. The questions asked in student feedback on capability programmes need to reflect capability-based quality concerns and the different roles involved in capability tutoring. Personal interviews and retrospective appraisals would give a better impression of the effectiveness of teacher support. Equally, institutions need to devise base-line criteria appropriate to a capability environment and consistent with the institution's mission statement.

Organizational issues
Regular weekly timetables and fixed staff/student contact hours sustain the beliefs that knowledge and skills are best dispensed in equal and regular doses, that education and learning are synonymous with classes and contact with teachers, and the worth of programmes of study can in Part Two be judged by the number of hours students spend under classroom instruction.

The capability approach is based on the very different principle that students are better motivated, understand more and achieve more if they are helped to manage their own learning. The teacher's role is also different, being more concerned with the provision of a supportive and rigorous environment within which students can take responsibility. Our correspondents make reference to being strait-jacketed by the even distribution of staff time. At the initial planning and negotiation stages, for instance, students may need frequent guidance, perhaps in small groups, or occasionally on an individual basis. In later stages, when they are pursuing their studies, their need for personal contact is much reduced and rises again when they are reviewing their achievements and progress.

A student case-load approach offers more flexibility and reflects the nature of the relationship between tutor and student. An annual (or termly) calculation of contact time allows peaks and troughs without an overall increase in staff activity. By front loading staff support, particularly with non-standard students, overall wastage rates can be reduced and the quality of student learning enhanced. Many staff enjoy intensive periods of work if as a consequence there are quieter periods for recharging or developing their own academic interests.

Resources for learning

Innovation has a resource dimension. Many of the changes reported to us have been made 'on-the-hoof' while teachers have been busy doing other things. Staff need time and support to work through entirely different ways of using scarce resources. The challenge to managers of HEIs and, indeed, funding bodies is to recognize the importance of the time and space required for rethinking and restructuring. Any major company would expect to have to invest in the design, development and appraisal of new products in addition to its normal staff development activities. One of the reasons for the success of the Enterprise in Higher Education Initiative in stimulating change has been its allocation of funds to release some staff time to develop new approaches. The individual amounts have been quite small and the return has been high.

Capability programmes encourage students to engage library and other learner resources directly. As teachers teach less, students use other resources more. Institutions help the introduction of capability programmes when their procedures for accessing computers, databases, photocopiers, videos and personal computers are readily open to students. Networked library services and computer-assisted learning facilities can give students access to a much wider range of specialist expertise than is available even within the best subject departments. Effective provision and use of a wide range of learning resources can free teachers to concentrate more on helping students talk through what they are doing. A number of the examples show how students are often able to secure specialist resources (often superior to those available in the HEI) from outside agencies as part of jointly negotiated projects. A teacher-dominated approach tends to confine students to using teacher provided materials.

Capability education involves a high priority being given to the development of systems (administrative and technical) for facilitating student access to learning resources of all kinds; it involves giving greater status to those responsible for managing the learning resources, via increasing their internal financial allocations and ensuring their membership of key committees, including those planning new programmes. If, as a consequence of being able to respond directly to the needs of individual students, learning quality rises and student attrition rates fall, investment in the expansion of the learning resources infrastructure is money well spent.

Institutional power structures

A major obstacle to change identified by many correspondents is an assumed reluctance on the part of boards of study and other key approving committees to sanction major changes in admissions, course structures and assessment methods. The previous section on the challenge for accrediting bodies gives some guidance on how the procedures for course approvals can aid the introduction of capability programmes. HEIs can assist further by reviewing the membership of those key committees.

One consequence of traditional promotion policies in the universities is that many senior positions have become occupied by those who have been most successful in academic research and publications rather than specialists in educational methods. One influence of the CNAA has been to stimulate expertise in curriculum development in the polytechnics and colleges. Their power structures reflect this, as do their internal procedures for quality assurance and programme validation. Consideration is given to the appropriateness of the intended learning outcomes; processes are discussed, as well as the content. The interrelatedness of academic and organizational change is addressed. Internal quality assurance procedures are increasingly a feature of the whole HE sector. If these new internal instruments remain in the control of groups primarily concerned with the preservation of their own definitions of subject relevance, their potential for stimulating education for capability may not be fully realized.

The challenge for employers

Our examples clearly illustrate that effective academic employer collaboration can be a significant factor in the development of student capability. Employers offer students opportunities to: (1) experience the demands of the work-place, (2) test their understanding of their college work through its application, (3) appreciate the importance of personal skills, (4) develop new skills and insights, (5) have access to specialist materials and equipment not normally available to students, (6) explore the relevance of their studies, and (7) taste possible future careers. Successful contacts with employers can give students a sound base on which to develop their college work and increase their motivation.

College/employer collaboration can be still more effective when students have direct involvement in the negotiations, and when all parties concerned are committed to using the placement for the educational development of the student. Some of the most interesting examples involve students shopping around for placements which give them the kinds of learning experiences they need and employers making sure that students have those experiences and receive constructive feedback. Time is found for reviewing student plans, progress and achievements with the students themselves; students are trusted in front-line activities, working with researchers or directly with clients. Placements are fully integrated with the college-based programme.

Capability placements work well for employers too. They get motivated students who have thought out why they want to be there. They get students who are useful, who are bringing college expertise to bear on problems within their own organizations. Employers have the opportunity to influence directly the student's learning and to spot talent for future employment. They are helping to raise the quality and relevance of higher education. By participating in student negotiated three-way learning contracts they replicate business life and prepare students for responsible self-development within the context of institutional goals.

Not all the experience reported to us is so good. When times are hard, some employers have to cut back on their involvement. Despite strong employer support for the development of capability (usually at higher management levels) commitment and understanding vary enormously, even within the same company. There is a major task to educate more employers about the meaning and need for capability and why their business will depend on having staff who can manage change and take responsibility for their own performance. Difficulties appear to be most acute at local levels where hard-pressed line managers desperately need to recruit people with skills for particular tasks, however short-lived the usefulness of those skills might be. Some major companies who advocate the development of capability still compete for people from prestigious universities or from popular courses without reference to the nature of the student's learning experiences. Many industrial representatives who collaborate with higher education see courses purely in content terms, and do not understand the importance of the learning process. Major businesses like banks, for instance, send their staff on highly structured lecture-based courses leading to professional qualifications when they could more effectively help their staff by negotiating learning contracts with the local college, giving them access to specialist tuition and resources to support their work-based professional development.

From our discussions with academics, students and employers the situation is improved when:

- employers monitor their recruitment patterns to see if they recruit from capability courses;
- recruiters ask how students used their higher education, set their own goals, monitored their own performance and managed their own learning;
- employers monitor the progress of recruits through their first years of employment according to their higher education experience and give constructive feedback to recruiters and colleges;
- employers educate their own staff about the kinds of qualities the company needs and the kinds of learning experiences which will help students develop them;
- employers give capable recruits responsible jobs to do, with opportunities and support for their further development;
- colleges stop asking 'what does industry need?' – industry as a whole does not have a clear or uniform answer – and start working in partnership with particular companies to help students negotiate their own appropriate programme and learning goals;
- colleges have the confidence to educate employers about the different ways they can educate students for employment and explain why capability approaches are in the employers' interests;
- colleges and employers get to know each other's business, as equal partners in developing personal and organizational effectiveness;
- employers serve on college committees and press for students to be given more responsibility and accountability for their own learning and ask how institutional mission statements are reflected in promotion and staff-appraisal policies;
- employers give their capability recruits the opportunity to set goals and manage their own progress;
- employers make their own expertise in staff development, staff appraisal and skills development more widely known and available to colleges;

- colleges involve employers in the supervision of student progress and in the assessment of student performance;
- large and prestigious companies take steps to educate smaller companies, including their own suppliers, about the importance of capability and the part they can play in its development;
- large and prestigious companies help to change the climate of opinion about the limitations of traditional forms of assessment and the validity of assessments based on what students can do with what they know;
- local Training and Enterprise Councils help smaller companies to arrange three-way learning contracts with students and colleges; and
- capable graduates explore the opportunities potential employers offer for continuing personal and professional development, and the chance to work with initiative and responsibility.

In recent years, higher education has been criticized for not adequately preparing students for the world of work. Higher education has taken those criticisms seriously, particularly, but not only, in the polytechnics and the newer universities. Many changes have been made and this book presents only a small sample of what is going on. Higher education has begun to understand its own role better by making it more explicit. Some good practice is long-standing and academics are beginning to understand and explain its relevance more effectively.

Employers have a responsibility to match the commitment of higher education. The capability approach offers real advantages to companies: flexible responses to rapidly changing educational needs; short lead-times for new courses; more effective partnerships; and better recruits. Capable recruits will help establish total quality management; they will help the company respond more effectively to changing circumstances. TQM companies could make use of capability focused validation and accreditation procedures in their local HEI to give intellectual support to their own internal staff-development activities and formal qualifications to their staff. The development of capability is in all our interests, and we all have a part to play in its promotion. Employers are in an excellent position to play a positive role and have the means to do so. Their interests go beyond the narrow demands of their own immediate recruitment needs; a capable society improves the quality of life of their employees and their customers.

The challenge for funding councils
The challenge for funding bodies is to find ways of rewarding those institutions aspiring to develop the capability of students and those who are achieving it. The experience of the Department of Employment's

Enterprise in Higher Education Initiative is that even small amounts of investment in staff time and staff development can bring about significant changes in staff attitudes and practice. Many of the examples brought to our attention have been stimulated or assisted by the EHE scheme.

Government funding of higher education institutions is now tied to external assessments of the quality of provision. The Higher and Further Education Funding Councils have the leverage to stimulate changes at very little cost. Two tools are available to them: the criteria used for the assessment of quality, and the targeting of funds for particular activities.

Criteria for judging quality
It would not make sense if the criteria used for the assessment of quality rewarded existing practice when one of the purposes of the new funding arrangements is to improve the quality and relevance of practice. There are a number of possible criteria which come into this category. There is little point, for instance, in giving extra rewards to institutions for expanding numbers according to fashionable subject titles such as business studies or technology if the student experience on those courses reinforces passive and dependent learning and does little to develop deeper levels of student understanding of the subject or promote their ability to act effectively in the wider world.

Quality judgements according to high A level scores may ignore the potential for rewarding the progress students make from modest beginnings to high achievement (ie, the value added through the quality of the service provided by the institution), and sustain the perpetuation of traditional styles of teaching (see the earlier section on the challenge for course designers).

Rewarding high first destination employment rates when employers compete for recruits from the more prestigious institutions without reference to the quality of their learning experiences may sustain those institutions whose previous generations of graduates have contributed to the general criticisms of the 'unworldliness' or lack of initiative of graduates as a whole.

Capability education will not be promoted if external assessments of quality consider the nature of the student's educational experience according to traditional views of teaching. In the absence of viable alternatives the former Polytechnics and Colleges Funding Council used the ratings of Her Majesty's Inspectorate (HMI), whose definitions of good quality include 'a well-organized purposeful programme of teaching...

lucid exposition... intelligent student response... provision of regular indications of student progress'.

Successfully taking responsibility for one's own learning, we argue, is a more rewarding and demanding educational experience than being responsive to purposeful teaching and appreciative of lucid teacher exposition. Being able to set, justify, negotiate and achieve one's own objectives within a rigorous environment, review one's own progress and demonstrate one's achievements against criteria negotiated with accrediting bodies and relevant employers is a better mark of quality than being able to receive and build on regular indications of progress from teachers, useful though such feedback and advice might be.

Moreover, HMI ratings are aggregated. Poor learning environments can mask otherwise good performance. Some of our correspondents complain that their innovations have had to be housed in marginal accommodation and have been developed at times of funding difficulties, which contributes to an overall environmental impression of low quality.

Student capability will not be enhanced if assessments of quality are based on student performance in predetermined, separately tested and objectively measurable personal skills and qualities. Capability is an integration of specialist expertise, personal skills, self-esteem and values and can only be satisfactorily demonstrated through the effectiveness and appropriateness of actions taken, the explanations given, the support and co-operation achieved, and the learning derived from the experience. Separate assessments of skills will perpetuate the difference between the possession of knowledge and skills and the ability to use them effectively.

Higher Education for Capability will be promoted if external assessments of quality consider:

- the relevance of an institution's aims or mission to the changing circumstances in the world outside, and the effectiveness of its internal procedures for ensuring their achievement;
- the extent to which students are encouraged to take responsibility and be accountable for significant aspects of their own learning;
- the effectiveness of the tutorial and institutional support for students taking responsibility and the responsiveness to their needs;
- the opportunities students have to relate their studies to their longer term employment or personal needs and aspirations;
- the commitment to promoting student learning from their experiences of being responsible and accountable and the rigour with which their learning achievements are judged;

- the effectiveness of any external participation in the planning, operation and assessment of student negotiated programmes;
- assessments of student performance based on the application of skills and knowledge, not just on the possession of knowledge; and
- the longer term career performance of graduates based on feedback from employers.

Targeted funds

All major businesses invest in product development. If the Funding Councils wish to use their resources to stimulate the introduction of new capability programmes, they could usefully target funds for particular activities. For instance, where institutions make specific commitments to the development of capability programmes, support should be given to pay for the time needed for the essential preliminary work. Funding normally follows student numbers; there are no students on courses under development. Plans not fulfilled could lead to penalties in later years.

Funds targeted on the development of learning resources infrastructures – including IT systems, computer-assisted learning, media resources, library materials and services, library and media resources staff, external links and study materials – will help reduce student dependence on tutors, widen the range of expertise available to students and prepare students for the high technology world they must eventually join. The availability of learning resources will make it easier for institutions to switch the emphasis of their courses to student responsibility and for staff to concentrate on the provision of 'critical dialogue' on the quality of student learning.

By giving priority to the development of capability programmes, the Funding Councils will also be helping institutions make effective provision for wider access into higher education. The greater the variety of student intake, the greater the need to make varied and flexible provision. As indicated in an earlier RSA report, *More Means Different* (Ball, 1989), the experience in the examples of capability programmes submitted to the RSA also indicates that 'different means more'. Programmes which relate directly to the individual experiences of students can reduce attrition rates and save resources.

Concluding remarks

Increasing numbers of people in all sections of higher education are working to improve the quality and relevance of student learning by giving students opportunities to be responsible and accountable for what they do. Many are breaking new ground; most are challenging the traditional view that quality education can consist entirely of a sequence of lectures to passive students, however well prepared and delivered the lectures might be. A new culture is being developed in which the roles of teachers, students, employers and institutional administrators merge into a common commitment to learning. The vision in the original *Education for Capability Manifesto* of combining the best features of 'education' and 'training' in the same process is becoming a reality for many students. Students are now developing the 'can do' as well as the 'know how'.

All of those involved in the preparation of this book hope that the examples presented and the issues raised will help our understanding of what educating for capability means in practice.

Acknowledgement
The section on the professional bodies was prepared with the assistance of James H. Armstrong, formerly a President of the Institute of Structural Engineers.

References
Ball, Sir Christopher (1989) *More Means Different*. London: RSA.
CNAA (1989) *CNAA Handbook, 1989*. Council for National Academic Awards.

Examples and Reports Submitted to the RSA

In compiling the specialist chapters in Part Two, the authors have drawn on reports of experiences submitted to the RSA by colleagues in the institutions listed below.

Higher Education for Capability would welcome details of other examples for inclusion in its National Capability and Enterprise Database for dissemination throughout the HE sector. Data submission forms can be obtained from the HEfC office at 20 Queen Square, Leeds LS2 8AF; Tel (0532) 347725; Facsimile (0532) 442025.

UNIVERSITY OF BATH
{1}   BSc/MEng in Electronic and Electrical Engineering, BEng/MEng in Electrical and Electronic Engineering for the European market, BEng in Electronic and Communication Engineering
{2}   School of Pharmacy and Pharmacology, Honours degree course with integrated scheme including communication skills

CITY OF BIRMINGHAM POLYTECHNIC
{3}   Polytechnic Certificate by Negotiated Study (Art & Design) and CNAA linked Awards: Certificate in Higher Education (Art & Design) and Diploma in Higher Education (Art & Design)
{4}   Diploma in Social Work leading to CQSW
{5}   BA (Hons) English Language and Literature

BOURNEMOUTH POLYTECHNIC
{6}   BA (Hons) Business Studies (CNAA) first year Computer Business Game
{7}   BTEC (HND) in business, finance and tourism
{8}   BEng (Hons) Electronic Systems Design (CNAA). Currently being developed BTEC/HND in Electronics Associated Common Skills Development – Self-Development, Self-Awareness, Personal Skills
{9}   BA/BSc Health and Community Studies (CNAA)
{10} BSc (Hons) Clinical Nursing (CNAA)

UNIVERSITY OF BRADFORD
{11} Two different four-year sandwich courses or three-year Hons sandwich courses leading to Hons degrees in Electrical and Electronic Engineering

and in Electronic, Computer and Communications Engineering, and one
full-time three-year Hons degree in Electrical Engineering
{12}   The Partnership Awards, Problem-Based Learning in Civil Engineering

BRADFORD AND ILKLEY COMMUNITY COLLEGE
{13}   BTEC HND/C Business and Finance and in Public Administration
{14}   A credit accumulation and transfer scheme (CAT) leading to awards of
       CNAA, from Sept '92 leading to BA (Hons), BEd (Hons), Dip. HE and
       Cert. HE from University of Bradford. Modularization of various BA
       (Hons) programmes

BRIGHTON POLYTECHNIC
{15}   BA (Hons) International Tourism Management
{16}   BSc (Hons)/Dip. HE. Mathematics for Management
{17}   BEng/MEng (Hons) in Mechanical Engineering, Business concepts
{18}   BA (Hons) Humanities – students acquiring, practising and being as-
       sessed according to transferable intellectual skills, hence oral assessment
       (course work and final exam) and small group teaching

BRISTOL POLYTECHNIC
{19}   BA (Hons) Systems Analysis: year four of sandwich course
{20}   BA Humanities degree. Modular degree
{21}   BA (Hons) Social Science Education for Capability

UNIVERSITY OF BUCKINGHAM
{22}   International Management Centres, MBA, action learning programme,
       part-time 18-month programme, teamwork, presentation skills, work-
       based project

UNIVERSITY OF CAMBRIDGE
{23}   PGCE (Secondary)

POLYTECHNIC OF CENTRAL LONDON
{24}   BSc Science (Biotechnology) Microbial & Molecular Genetics

CITY UNIVERSITY
{25}   Computational Mathematics and final year projects

COVENTRY POLYTECHNIC
{26}   BEng (Hons) Engineering (Combined Engineering Studies)
{27}   BEng (Hons) and degree course in Engineering, module B81 Small Busi-
       ness Enterprise year two
{28}   BSc degree and Hons degree. Method of teaching problem-solving to
       undergraduate engineering students and assessment of group projects
{29}   BEng (Hons) Manufacturing Systems Engineering
{30}   Final year course in Industrial Geography
{31}   BSc Geography

CREWE AND ALSAGER COLLEGE OF HIGHER EDUCATION
{32} BA (Hons) Applied Social Studies – by independent study (full-time and part-time)

DERBYSHIRE COLLEGE OF HIGHER EDUCATION
{33} HND Computer Studies, year two controlling module, Systems Analysis

UNIVERSITY OF DUNDEE
{34} BEng (Hons) Civil Engineering, CE225, second year project, project-based class
{35} Centre for Medical Education, Assessment of Practical Skills: The Objective Structured Practical Examination (OSPE)

UNIVERSITY OF DURHAM
{36} Business School: Diploma in Enterprise Management
{37} Numeracy Project

UNIVERSITY OF EAST ANGLIA
{38} Development of University English Teaching Project (DUET) research and teaching project organized on a workshop basis
{39} BSc (Hons) degree in Environmental Sciences or Ecology

POLYTECHNIC OF EAST LONDON
{40} BA (Hons) Fashion: Design with Marketing
{41} PG Diploma: Business for Fashion
{42} BA (Hons) Fine Art
{43} One-year full-time HITECC/Foundation programme as first year of four-year degree or three-year higher diploma comprising four components (Eng 19)
{44} BSc (Hons) New Technology (Interdisciplinary Studies)
{45} Certificate in Planning for Professional Development

EDGE HILL COLLEGE OF HIGHER EDUCATION
{46} BSc (Hons) in Organization and Management Studies
{47} PGCE Upper Primary Course

UNIVERSITY OF EDINBURGH
{48} Faculty of Science and Engineering, Biology Teaching Organization, Enterprise Skills Project

UNIVERSITY OF ESSEX
{49} Learning to Learn in Technology – programming and software engineering
{50} Undergraduate History Project

UNIVERSITY OF EXETER
{51} Open Learning Module, second year of core course

{52} BA (Hons) Teacher Education Teaching Practice, preparation and supervision

{53} BSc/BA (Ed) Educational Studies

{54} School of Education: three books offering a standard undergraduate maths course in (i) number theory, (ii) geometrical groups and (iii) real analysis, each in the form of a sequence of 800 problems with summaries, history, outline solutions and notes

GLASGOW POLYTECHNIC
{55} BA (Hons) Social Studies

UNIVERSITY OF GLASGOW (Robert Clark Centre of Technological Education)
{56} Technology Design Workshop

{57} A four-year BTechEd Technology Design Workshops

GOLDSMITHS COLLEGE, UNIVERSITY OF LONDON
{58} Diploma in Experiential Learning

{59} BEd Professional Studies Course

HATFIELD POLYTECHNIC
{60} Business School: BA (Hons) Business Studies, Business Problems Analysis: An integrated skills development course

{61} Electrical and Electronic Engineering, a design project, first year

{62} Electrical and Electronic Engineering, the Marconi Lectures, second year

{63} Interdiscipliniary design project for all second year Engineers, BEng Electrical and Electronic Engineering

HOMERTON COLLEGE CAMBRIDGE
{64} Modern languages PGCE Student Teacher Project

HUDDERSFIELD POLYTECHNIC
{65} School of Business: BA (Hons) Business Studies

{66} BA (Hons)/BA Computing in Business

{67} BA (Hons) Historical and Political Studies, politics seminar course

UNIVERSITY OF HULL
{68} Group Projects in Software Engineering

HUMBERSIDE POLYTECHNIC
{69} Humberside Business School: A computerized business simulation as part of the first year in a number of BA couses in management

{70} Degree in Social and Professional Studies – DipHE modules

{71} BA (Hons) Contemporary Studies, student research consortium

{72} BA (Hons) Contemporary Studies

IMPERIAL COLLEGE OF SCIENCE AND TECHNOLOGY, UNIVERSITY OF LONDON
{73} Mechanical Engineering Building, Pimlico Connection Tutoring Scheme (Eng 42)
{74} Problem-based course to run alongside conventionally taught courses in the third year of mechanical engineering degree programme

UNIVERSITY OF KENT AT CANTERBURY
{75} Rutherford College: four-year single Hons degree in Drama and Theatre Studies
{76} Part I course 'Advanced Italian' (post A level)
{77} Biochemistry second year degree course, Medical Aspects of Metabolism
{78} Diploma and MA in Continuing Education

KING ALFRED'S COLLEGE, WINCHESTER
{79} Getting Results and Solving Problems – The GRASP Project

KINGSTON POLYTECHNIC
{80} BA (Hons) Fine Art
{81} Foundation Course in Design
{82} BA (Hons) English, BA (Hons) History and BA (Hons) French Studies
{83} BA Modern Arts in History (Hons) second and third year: 'International Conflict and Co-operation 1815–1914'

LANCASHIRE POLYTECHNIC
{84} BA (Hons) in Hospitality Management (in conjunction with Blackpool and The Fylde College)

LANCASTER UNIVERSITY
{85} The Management School: Master of Arts in Management Learning (full-time); (course brochure)
{86} 'Creating the Managerial Portfolio: Building on Competency Approaches to Management Development' (CSML): MPhil Dissertation, (CSML) 'Projects in Management Development – The Worst of Both Worlds?'

LEEDS POLYTECHNIC
{87} BA (Hons) Graphic Design
{88} BA (Hons) Public Relations
{89} Post Graduate Diploma/MSc, Information Systems/Software Engineering route
{90} The Certificate in Community Studies
{91} Three Dimensional Design BA (Hons) Product Design Section, collaborative design development project with business/management students
{92} PG Diploma/ MSc Education Management

UNIVERSITY OF LEEDS
{93}   Design Course in year two, of a four-year MEng degree in Architectural Engineering
{94}   BSc (Hons) Physics with Electronics and Instrumentation. Individual and pair experimental project work with local industry
{95}   BSc (Hons) Physics with Electronics and Instrumentation. First year 'studio style' integrated lecture/laboratory course
{96}   Final year project for BSc (Hons) Animal Science and BSc (Hons) Animal Nutrition and Physiology

LEICESTER POLYTECHNIC
{97}   Leicester Business School: Diploma in Marketing (four modules for graduate entry) for part-time students in full-time occupations
{98}   Leicester Business School: BA (Hons) Business Studies, (BABS) (Business Decisions and Policy Making Component)
{99}   Leicester Business School: Part-time MBA Strategic Management option, final year
{100} Leicester Business School: Part-time DMS (Diploma in Management Studies)
{101} Leicester Business School and the School of Mechanical and Production Engineering: Running a business, module of first year degree course
{102} Law Clinic: optional activity for second and third year students
{103} BA (Hons) Arts and Humanities
{104} BA/BSc (Hons) Combined Studies
{105} BSc/BSc (Hons) Combined Studies, BSc/BSc (Hons) Science and the Environment, BSc/BSc (Hons) Biotechnology. One-year sandwich placement in all three courses
{106} BSc/BSc (Hons) Science and the Environment degree programme. A residential field course in introductory ecology
{107} BTEC Higher National Diploma in Science (Applied Biology)
{108} BSc (Hons) Biotechnology and others.
{109} BSc/BSc (Hons) Applied Chemistry. BSc/BSc (Hons) Chemistry or BSc/BSc (Hons) Physics with Business Studies. BTEC HND in Chemistry

UNIVERSITY OF LEICESTER
{110} First year Physical Chemistry Team Project
{111} Final year Inorganic Chemistry Research Project

UNIVERSITY OF LONDON
{112} Centre for Higher Education Studies: 'Making History Students Enterprising: Independent Study at Manchester Polytechnic'

MANCHESTER INSTITUTE OF SCIENCE AND TECHNOLOGY
{113} BSc (Hons) Textile Design Management, BSc (Hons)

MANCHESTER POLYTECHNIC
{114} Master's Programme in Management, by action learning and research. Managing by degree, a three-phase programme extending over two years
{115} MSc Management by action learning
{116} Module: The Competent Manager, currently in the preliminary stages

{117} The Business Consultancy Project Programme: central element of second year of HND in Business and Finance, and the fourth (final) year of the BSc (Hons) Business degree

{118} BA (Hons) Humanities/Social Studies and BA (Hons) Historical Studies

{119} BSc/BSc (Hons) Applied Biological Sciences

{120} PG Dip/MSc in Education Management

{121} BEd (Hons) Primary Training: Special Subject Drama

UNIVERSITY OF MANCHESTER

{122} Proposal for a three-tier system of education: ordinary BSc/Hons BSc/MSc/PhD

{123} Degree in Pharmacy. Vacational training programme in professional environment

MIDDLESEX POLYTECHNIC

{124} The Business Awareness Programme, part of the BA (Hons) programmes in Constructed Textiles, Printed Textiles and Fashion

{125} Middlesex Business School: BA Business Studies (BABS), a four-year sandwich course

{126} Middlesex Business School: A two-year enterprise workshop programme – company-based problem solving

{127} Middlesex Business School: Group-based peer-assessment, second year enterprise workshop programme (BABS)

{128} Partnership Awards 1991: Prize 21 Enterprise Skills through the Humanities. Nomination of humanities and social sciences faculties' development office for devising and organizing Middlesex Polytechnic Writers' Days

{129} Literature and Philosophy degree: submission made to a working party for the development of a new pedagogy for the degree

{130} The Writing and Publishing course as part of the BA (Hons) Humanities Modular Degree Scheme

MORAY HOUSE COLLEGE

{131} Experiment conducted over two years with course members studying for the Postgraduate Diploma in Linguistics and English Language Teaching (PGLELT)

{132} PGCE (Secondary) Chemistry Component

NEWCASTLE UPON TYNE POLYTECHNIC

{133} BA (Hons) Design for Industry

{134} BA (Hons) Fine Art

{135} BA (Hons) Fashion Marketing

UNIVERSITY OF NEWCASTLE UPON TYNE

{136} BEng in Marine Technology, second year, Engineers in Systems – an accomplishment-orientated model

{137} BEng (Hons) in Marine Technology

{138} Engineering Foundation year: first year of integrated four-year BEng or five-year MEng (Hons) degree course

THE POLYTECHNIC OF NORTH LONDON

{139} BA (Hons) Film Studies (Combined), part of the BA Humanities degree
{140} The Business School: Business Workshop, year one module
{141} BTEC HND in Science (Polymer Technology)
{142} IT and Work Environment, part of HND in Information Technology
{143} BA (Hons) Film Studies (Combined), part of BA Humanities degree
{144} Issues in Community Health Care SH301
{145} Dept of Applied Chemistry and Life Sciences, first year chemistry course
       leading to a BSc (Hons)
{146} BEd (Hons) year: Teaching practice, skills and competency preparation

NORTHERN COLLEGE OF EDUCATION, ABERDEEN

{147} Postgraduate Diploma Primary Education (early education)

NOTTINGHAM POLYTECHNIC

{148} BA (Hons) Humanities. New unitized course within a structured scheme
       currently in its second year.
{149} Diploma in Industrial Studies running in parallel with BSc Applied
       Chemistry degree
{150} BEd (Hons) Secondary Design & Technology

OPEN UNIVERSITY

{151} Advanced Diploma in Educational Management: Applied Studies in Edu-
       cational Management

OPEN UNIVERSITY IN SCOTLAND

{152} Learning skills course: learner-centered and directed, five two-hour work-
       shops over space of Open University academic year, involving students
       from all levels and across all faculties

OXFORD POLYTECHNIC

{153} BSc/BSc (Hons) Hotel and Catering Management (CNAA) Modular
{154} The modular degree course leading to BA (Hons) – specifically the
       course component in Post-war British Drama.
{155} Dept of Social Studies, modules Sociological Analysis I and II, Teaching
       Research Methods, part of the BA/BSc (Hons) Modular Degree Scheme
{156} Diploma in Planning, the final year of a four-year course. BA (Hons)
       given after three years: BA and Diploma together lead to professional
       recognition. MSc/Diploma in Urban Planning, the equivalent at postgrad-
       uate level
{157} Part of The TEED Programme for 'Widening Access to Higher Educa-
       tion, Science and Maths' managed by FOCUS Consultancy Ltd.

PAISLEY COLLEGE OF TECHNOLOGY

{158} BSc (Hons) Technology and Management: traditional four-year Hons de-
       gree course with an option to take a thick sandwich element at end of sec-
       ond year

{159} BSc or BSc (Hons) in Mathematical Sciences or Applicable Maths with Computing

PARSON CROSS COLLEGE, SHEFFIELD
{160} Certificate in Training and Development. Diploma in Training Management. Professional and Industrial Studies Programme

UNIVERSITY OF READING
{161} BSc (Hons) Agricultural Economics. Parts one and three, Farm Business Management module
{162} BEd (Hons) Economic & Industrial Understanding & the Primary School Curriculum

ROFFEY PARK MANAGEMENT COLLEGE
{163} A University of Sussex validated MBA

ST ANDREW'S COLLEGE OF EDUCATION
{164} Teaching Fellowship for Higher Grade Computing Studies

COLLEGE OF ST MARK & ST JOHN, PLYMOUTH
{165} BA (Hons) Modular Degree Programme: Recreation & Community and Creative Design. From 1992 Art & Design, with alternative joint majors, Media Studies, Public Relations or Recreation & Community

ST LUKE'S, EXETER
{166} PGCE Secondary

UNIVERSITY OF SALFORD
{167} Management Development Unit: BSc Electrical/Electronic Engineering
{168} BSc (Hons) in Finance and Accounting. Courses include: Financial Information Systems and Business Decision Taking
{169} Centre for Small Business Research: A two-year teaching company programme
{170} BSc (Hons) Modern Languages and Marketing Studies
{171} BSc (Hons) Business Studies, BSc (Hons) Modern Languages and Marketing Studies

SHEFFIELD CITY POLYTECHNIC
{172} Sheffield Business School: part-time MBA, strategy group project, final year
{173} BA (Hons) Accounting and Management Control: Financial Decision Making option
{174} BEng (Hons) in Integrated Engineering
{175} BEng (Hons) four-year sandwich course, Integrated Engineering; development and use of a portfolio system and associated progress scheme to show professional, personal and technical development

{176} Science Curriculum Initiatives and Learning Strategies (SCILS)
{177} Joint MEd degree dissertation
{178} Primary Conversion Course
{179} Diploma in Counselling.
{180} PGCE The Learning Record
{181} Negotiating and Contracting BEd (Hons) year two

UNIVERSITY OF SHEFFIELD
{182} Management School: Pilot scheme, self-evaluation, with help from Enter-
       prise Unit and Sheffield Polytechnic
{183} Global Political Economy and the Third World
{184} Enterprise Unit: EHE Curriculum Development Projects
{185} PGCE (Secondary) Collaborative Enquiry Element

SOUTH BANK POLYTECHNIC
{186} BSc (Hons) in Engineering Product Design
{187} MSc (Unit based) in Urban Engineering, Management Skills and Man-
       agement Development
{188} Course in Data Communications and Systems Software

UNIVERSITY OF SOUTHAMPTON
{189} MSc in Rehabilitation Studies

POLYTECHNIC SOUTH WEST
{190} Plymouth Business School: BTEC HND in Business and Finance
{191} Plymouth Business School: BA (Hons) Business Studies, with French,
       German or Spanish; BA (Hons) International Business with German,
       French or Spanish; BA (Hons) Personnel Management; BA (Hons) Mar-
       keting
{192} Plymouth Business School: BA Business Studies; 'The Great Poly Pic-
       ture Show' – an innovative approach to developing group working skills
{193} Satellite Training and Education Projects Uplink (STEPUP)
{194} BEng (Hons) in Civil Engineering Studies, Construction Management,
       year two
{195} HND in Civil Engineering Studies, year one, Construction
{196} HND in Rural Resource Management
{197} Department of Psychology, Visits Programme, year two optional skills
       course (part of EHE programme)
{198} BSc option modules in year two in Physical Oceanography and Marine
       Pollution, Diploma Hydrographic Survey, funding from TEED and
       CNAA

STAFFORDSHIRE POLYTECHNIC
{199} The Management Centre: Certificate in Management, based on National
       Management Standards (M I Level)
{200} BA (Hons) International Relations and BA (Hons) Modern Studies: simu-
       lation exercises
{201} BA (Hons) Literary and Historical Studies: course component Philos-
       ophy and Public Affairs
{202} BA (Hons) Literature and History, a case study

{203} 'Project Labcare', a project in HNC/HND Physics, HNC/HND Chemistry and BA Graphic Design (Audio Visual option)

UNIVERSITY OF STRATHCLYDE
{204} Centre for Academic Practice: Industry Studies, Hons year option
{205} BEng in Electronic and Electrical Engineering and BEng/BSc in Information Engineering, third year course in Application Specific Integrated Circuit (ASICS) Design
{206} Business School, Department of Information Science and the Centre for Academic Practice Postgraduate Diploma in Information, Library Studies and Information Management

SUFFOLK COLLEGE
{207} Research and Development Unit, DipHE and Degree by Independent Study (Managed by the Integrated Programme Unit [IPU])

SUNDERLAND POLYTECHNIC
{208} BTEC HND Visual Information Design Course (Interpretive Design)
{209} Business School: MBA programme, skills development and self-development programme
{210} Sunderland Business School: BTEC HND Business and Finance; Community and Business Support Services Ltd (CABSS) – a course owned company
{211} Sunderland Business School: courses and programmes in Quality Management, Polytechnic Diploma in Quality Assurance for the Pharmaceutical Industry
{212} A Proposal for internationally validated qualifications for Common Certificate of European Studies, one-year Diploma in European Studies and four-year degree in European Studies
{213} BEd Business Education

TEESSIDE POLYTECHNIC
{214} BSc (Hons) Psychology, BTEC HND/C Public Administration: structured personal tutoring
{215} Management Skills Course – Development of MGT Competences
{216} BTEC HND/C Public Administration
{217} BA (Hons) Humanities (Modular), syndicated learning in a contemporary literature course

THAMES POLYTECHNIC
{218} BA (Hons) Humanities

UNIVERSITY COLLEGE, UNIVERSITY OF LONDON
{219} Single Hons and combined, and MA in French

POLYTECHNIC OF WALES
{220} BSc (Hons) Technology and Business Studies
{221} Postgraduate Certificate in Teaching and Learning

UNIVERSITY COLLEGE OF WALES, ABERYSTWYTH
{222} Television Drama and Television Practical
{223} Introduction of business-related subjects to first year students through the medium of Welsh
{224} MSc by Distance Learning, Information Systems and Services for Health Care

UNIVERSITY COLLEGE OF WALES, BANGOR
{225} Applications Software, lecture/laboratory-based course introducing students to the basic uses of computers
{226} School of Education pilot scheme for self-development diaries
{227} Information about survey of Innovation in Mathematics courses in UK universities and polytechnics conducted by London Mathematical Society

WALLIS (Fashions)
{228} Industrial placement scheme

UNIVERSITY OF WARWICK
{229} Programme run jointly by History Department and History of Art Programme
{230} BA (QTS) Lifelong Learning and the School Curriculum

WESTMINSTER COLLEGE
{231} PGCE Primary and Secondary

WOLVERHAMPTON POLYTECHNIC
{232} BA(Hons) Visual Communication.
{233} The Enterprise Design Studio, part of the Visual Communication course.
{234} HND Design Communications
{235} 3D Design in Wood, Metals and Plastics; BA (Hons)
{236} Wolverhampton Business School: BA (Hons) Business Studies, BA (Hons) European Business Administration
{237} BSc (Hons) Business Information Systems; BSc (Hons) Business and Manufacturing systems; Law Option module: first semester of four-year BSc/BSc (Hons) courses
{238} BSc (Hons) Computer Science
{239} BSc (Hons) Computer Science, Business Information Processing 4 (BIP4)
{240} MSc course in Construction Management, Construction Simulation Game
{241} BSc (Hons) Computer Science, year four module: Business Information Processing 4 (Eng31)
{242} Disabled into Construction, one-year course to provide vocational training for disabled people
{243} BSc (Hons) Computer Science, BSc (Hons) Business Information Systems, MSc Information Technology, part-time and full-time modes, any year

{244} BSc (Hons) Computer Science year four, Business Information Processing 4 modules

{245} PG Dip/MA Communications Planning, postgraduate programme orientated to professional development

{246} BA (Hons) Cultural Studies Enterprise Modules - part of the Modular Degree Scheme

{247} Medical and Veterinary Parasitology, second and third year students, BSc/BSc (Hons), BEd

{248} The Modular Degree and Diploma Scheme leading to BA (Hons) in the various relevant subjects

{249} 'A Capability Approach to Language Teaching' Workshop

{250} Certificate in Health Education, validated by the Health Education Authority and CNAA

{251} Applied Biology Group: Module Medical and Veterinary Parasitology

{252} BTEC HND courses in Chemistry and Biology

{253} BSc (Hons), BEd Applied Pharmacology and Toxicology

{254} Modular INSET Programme

{255} BEd (Hons) Primary: Religious Studies option

{256} BEd (Hons) Primary: Modular Degree and Diploma Scheme

{257} The Further, Adult and Higher Education Professional Development Programme (FAHE) Cert Ed (FE) and PGCE (FE) BSc Nursing Education

{258} BEd (Hons) Secondary: Design and Technology, Business Studies, Maths, Modern Languages

WORCESTER COLLEGE OF HIGHER EDUCATION
{259} BA (Hons) Combined Studies: Social Science

Index